TUCK AND ROLL

GOST

TUCK AND ROLL

J HOUSTON

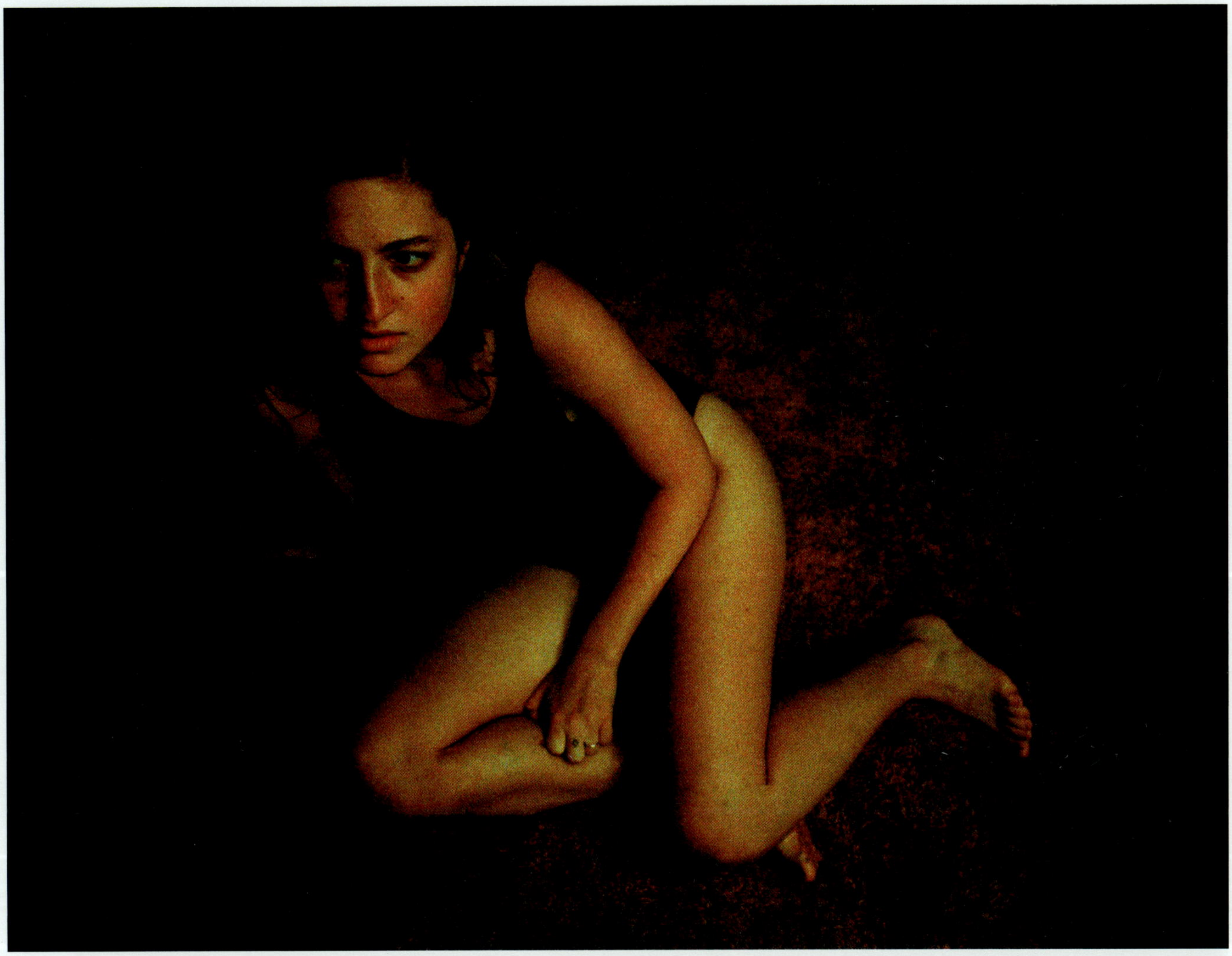

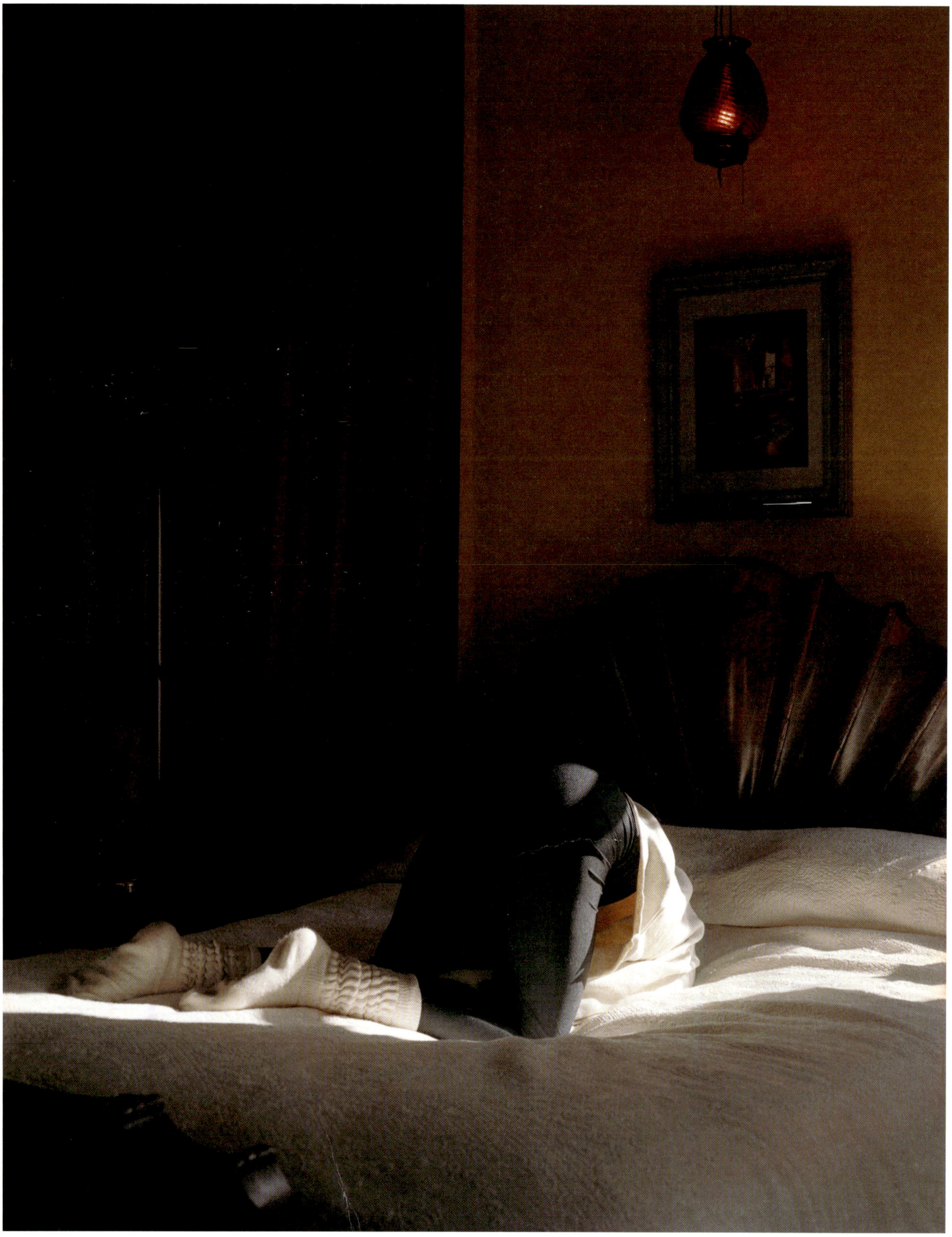

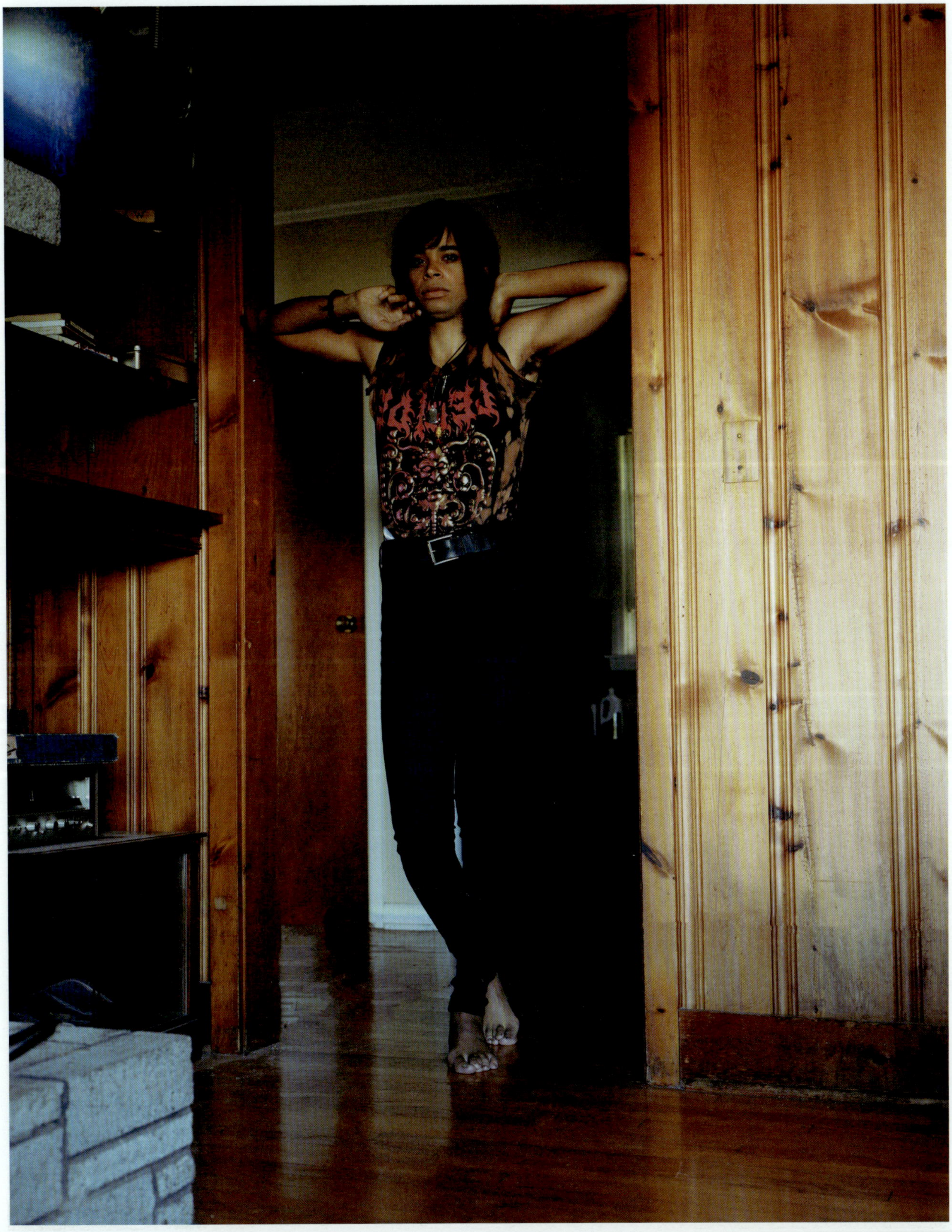

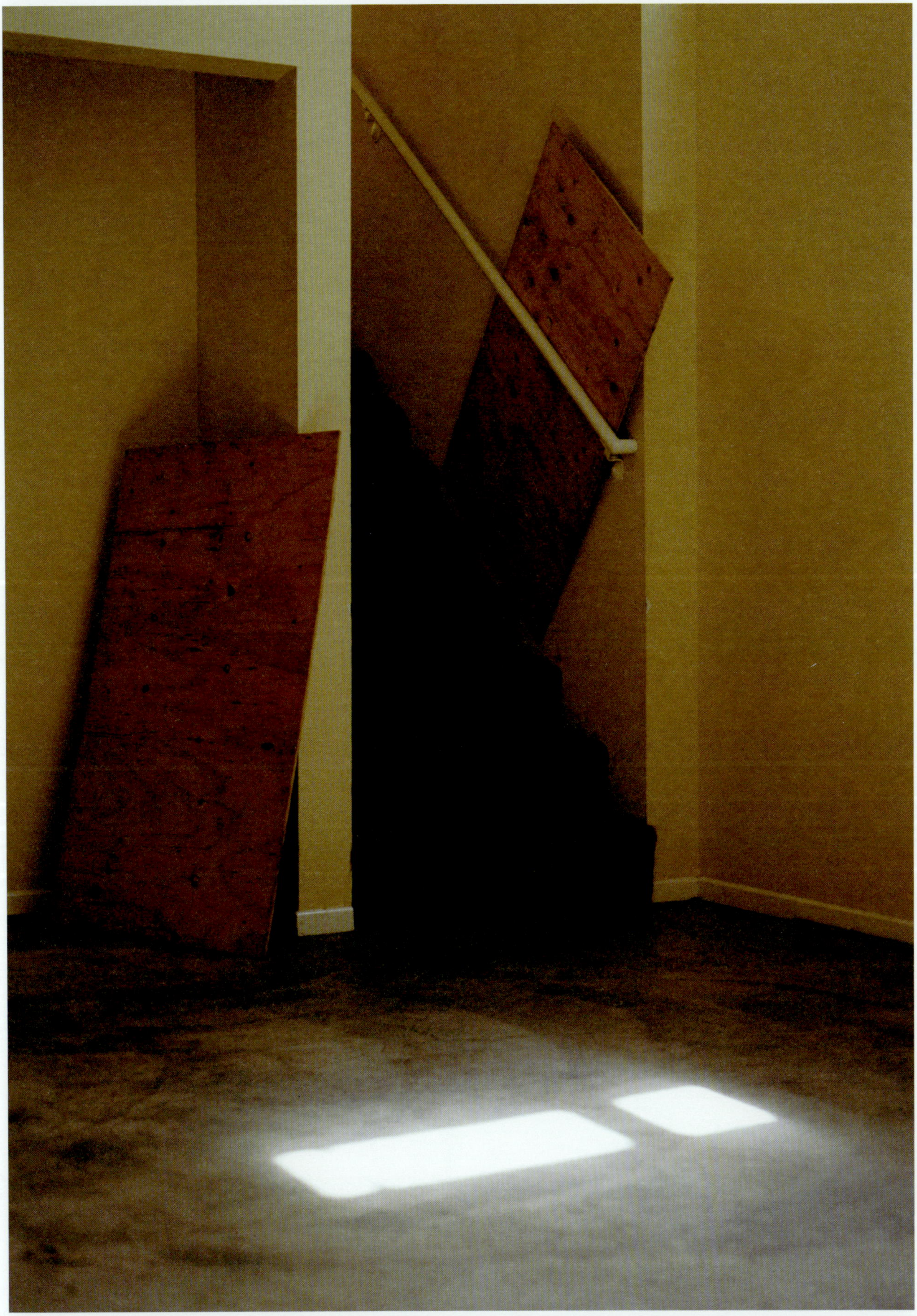

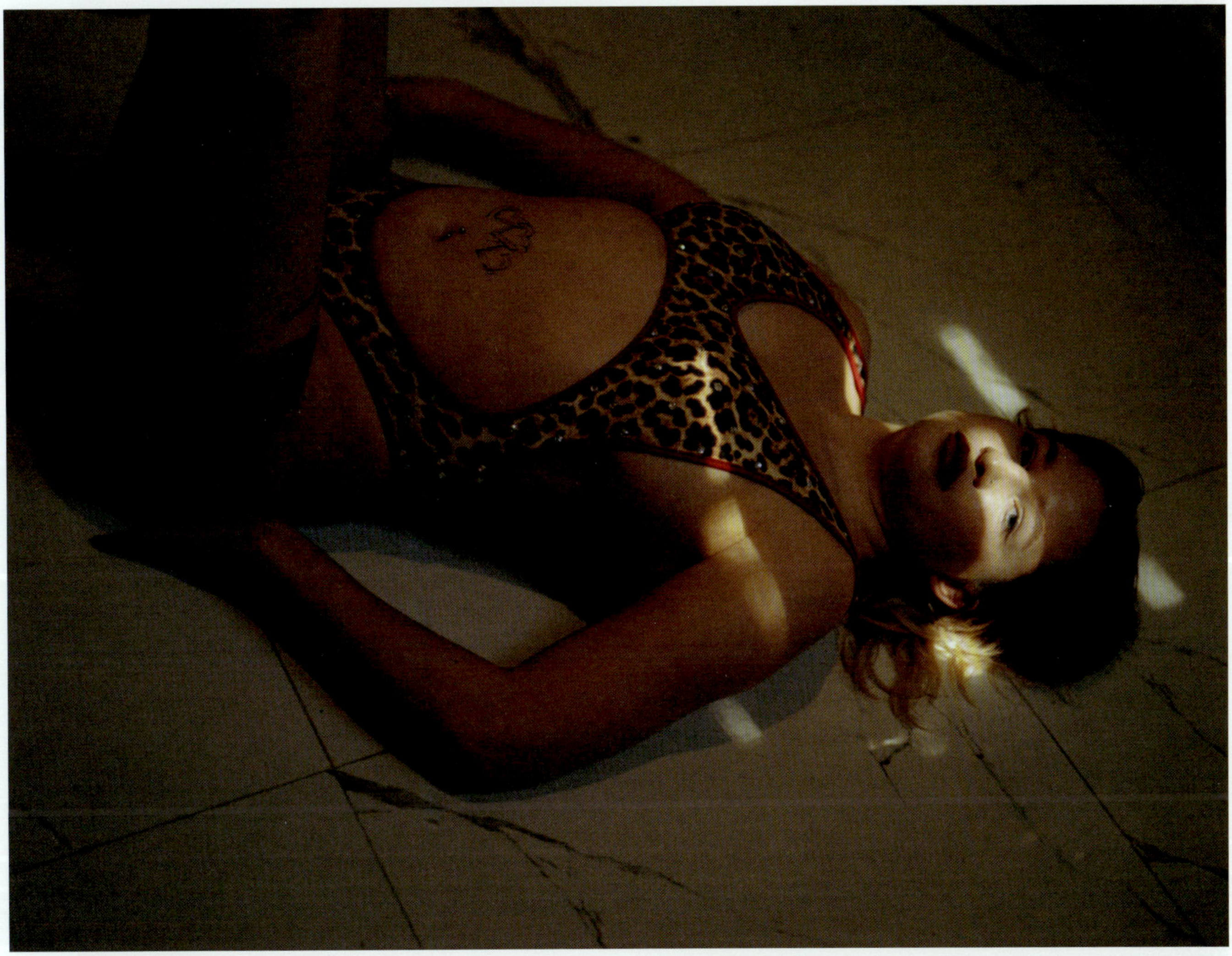

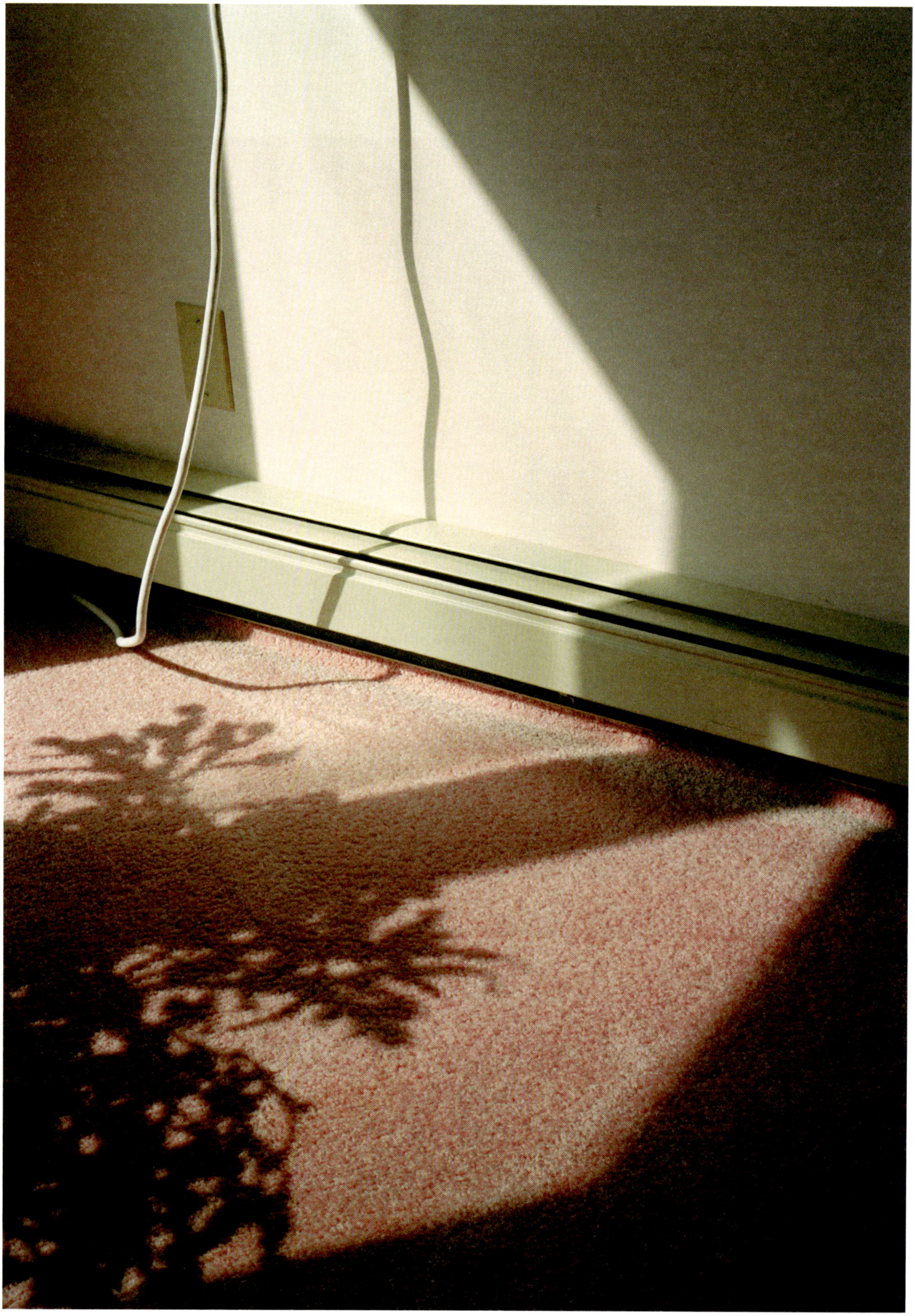

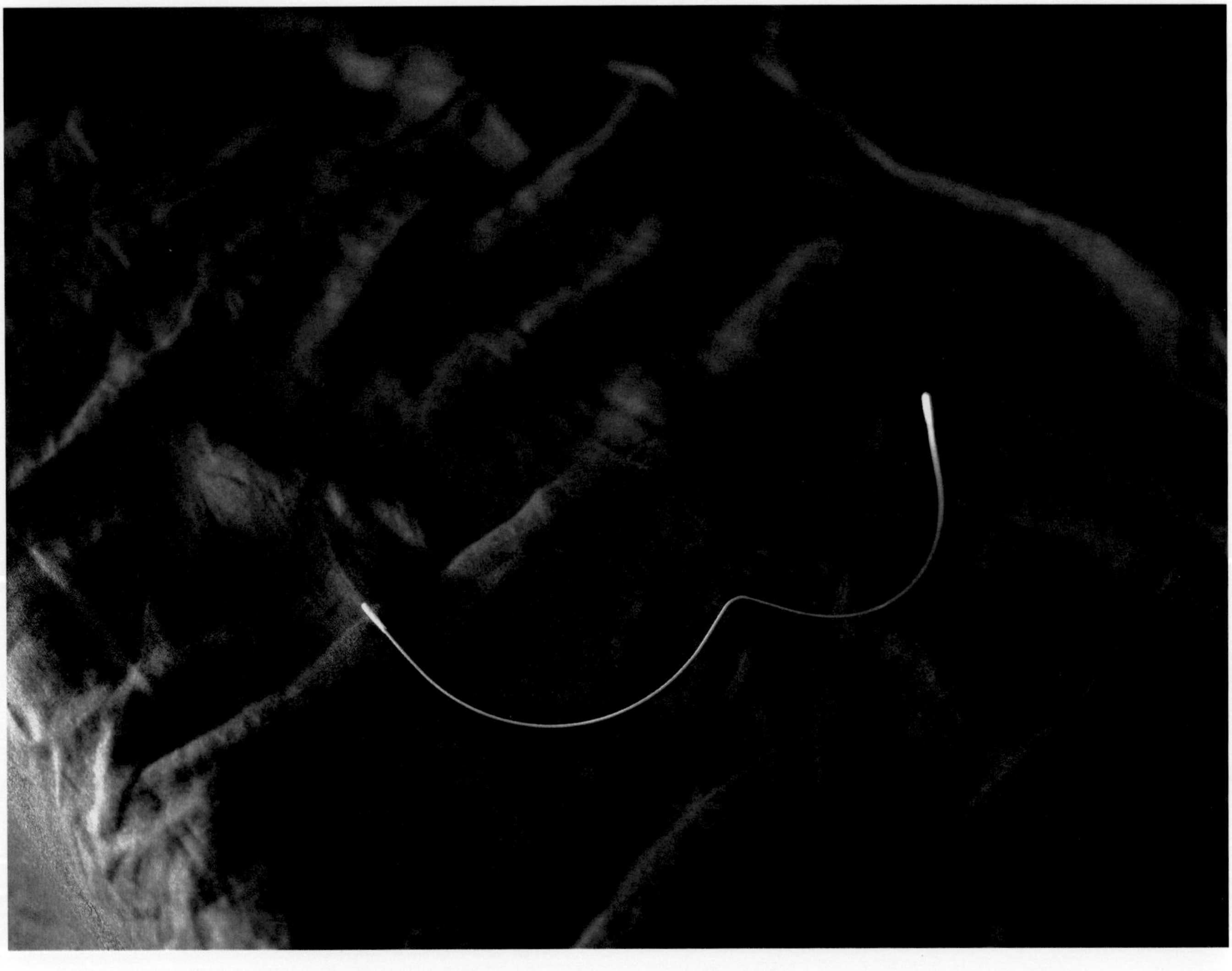

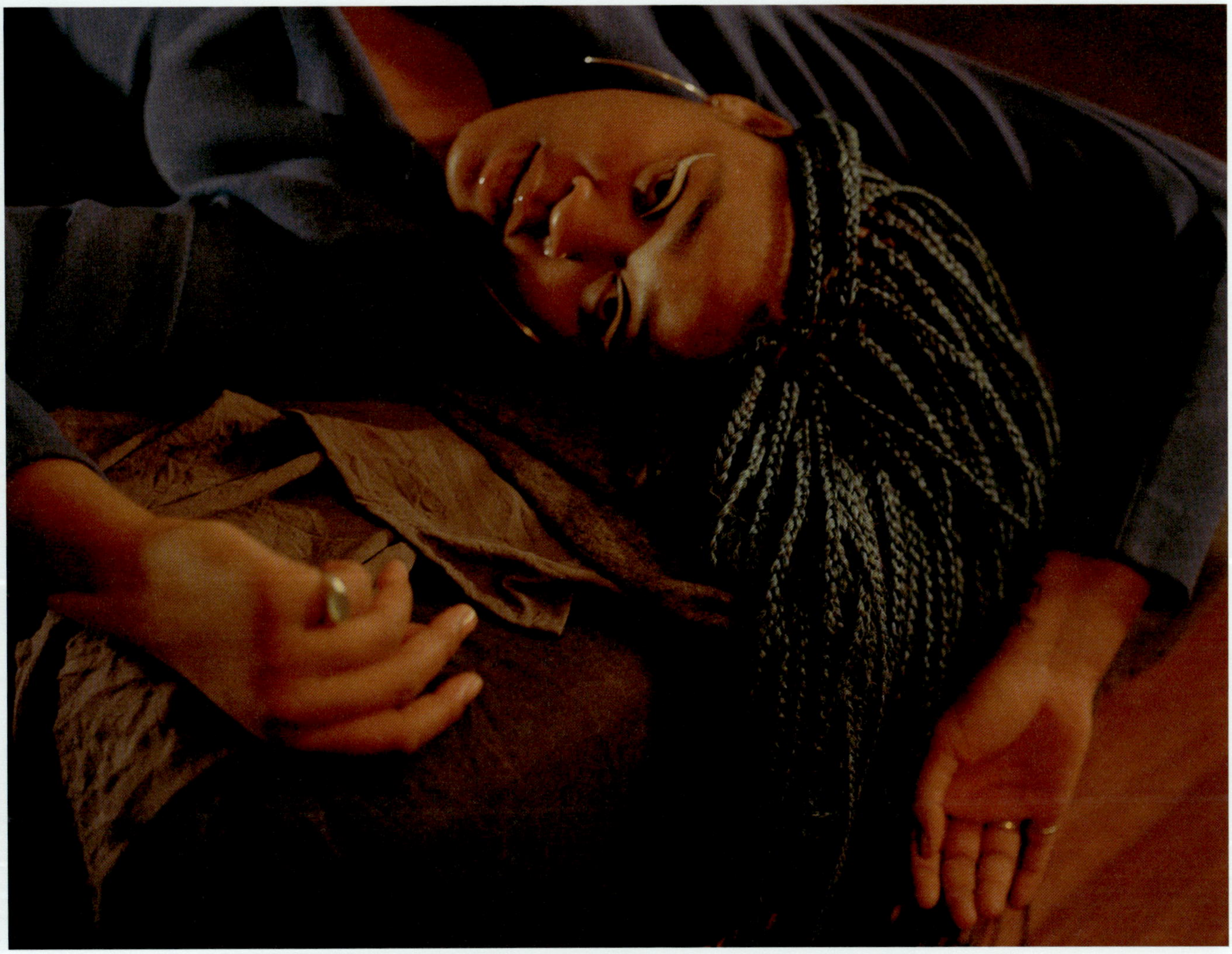

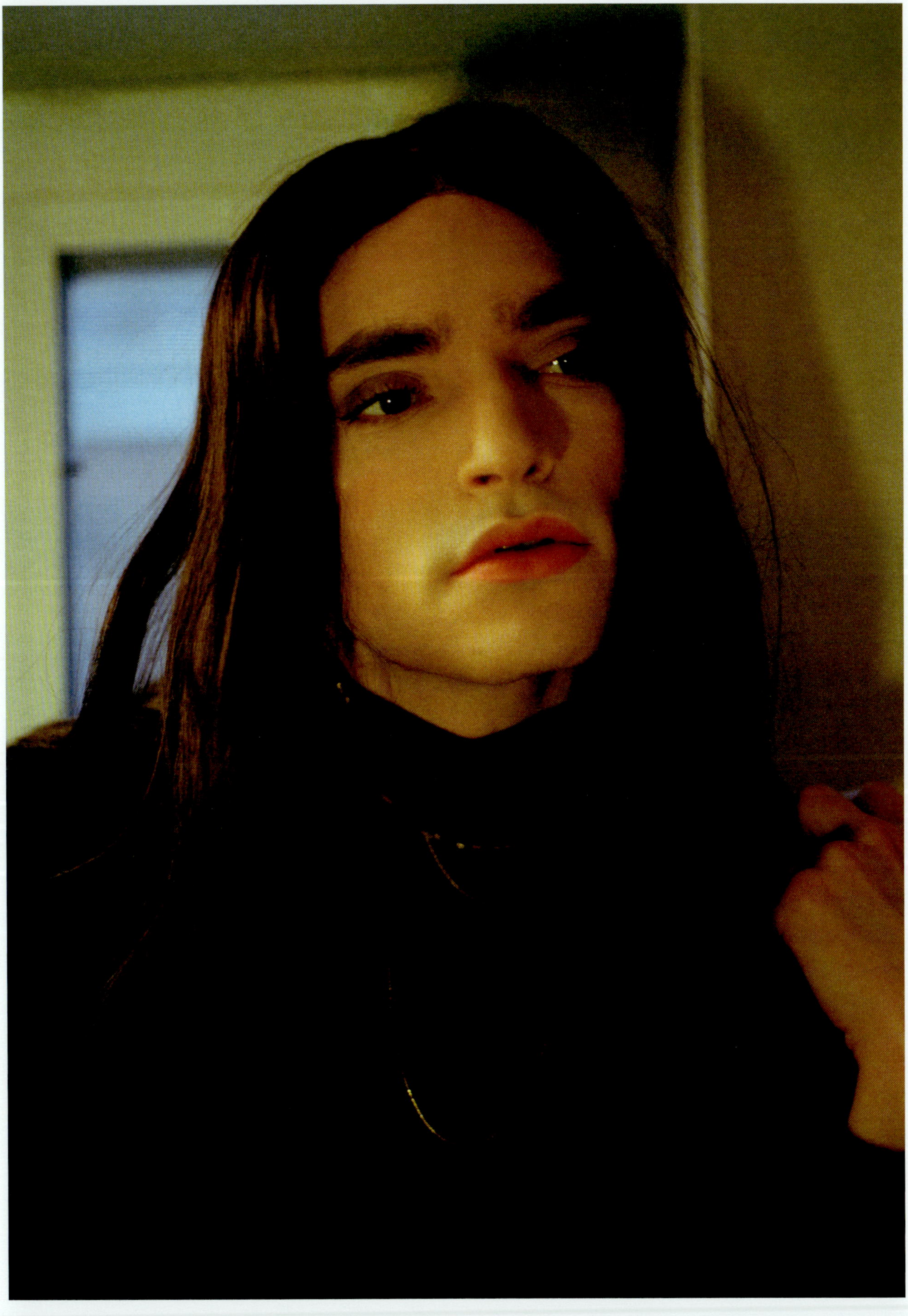

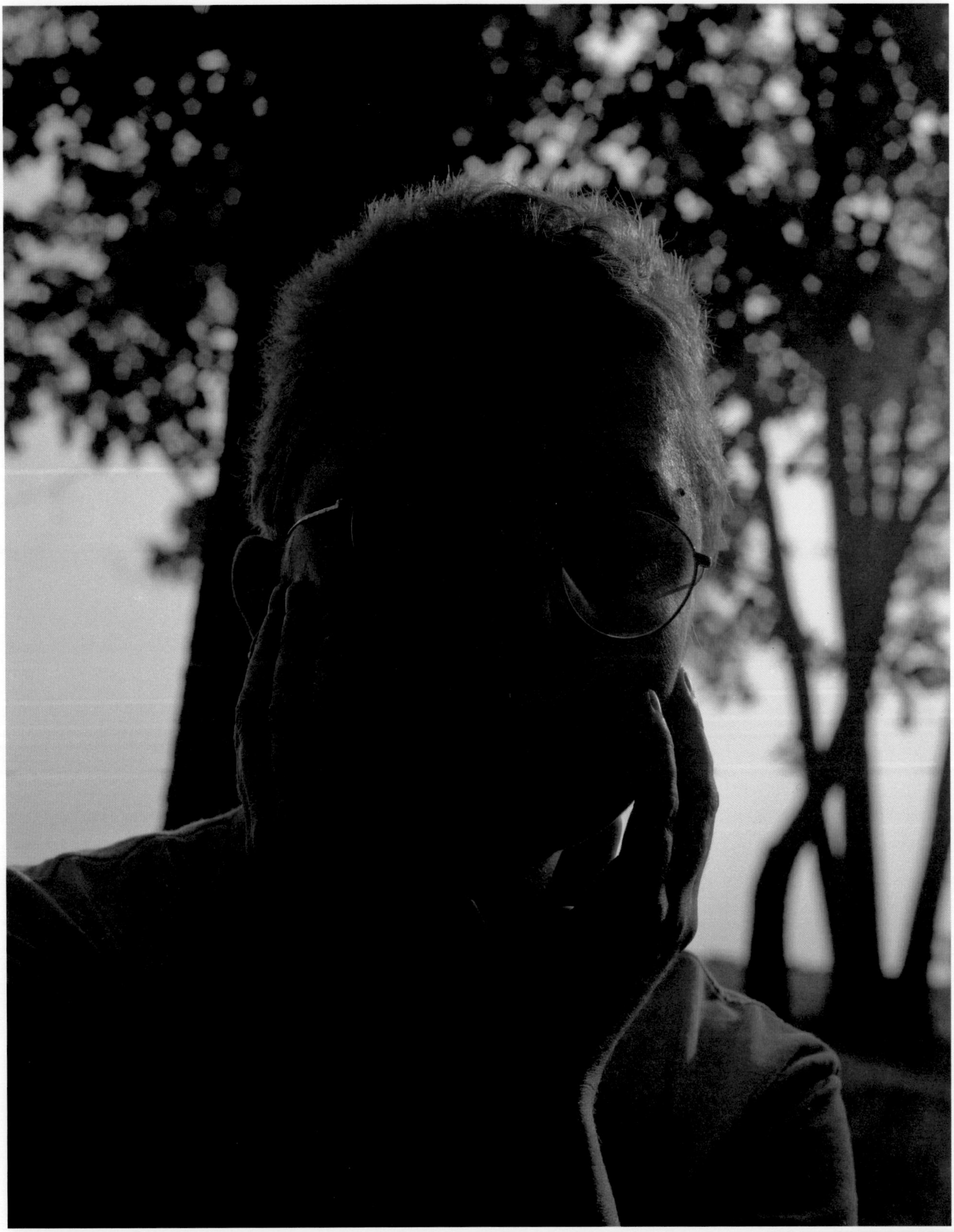

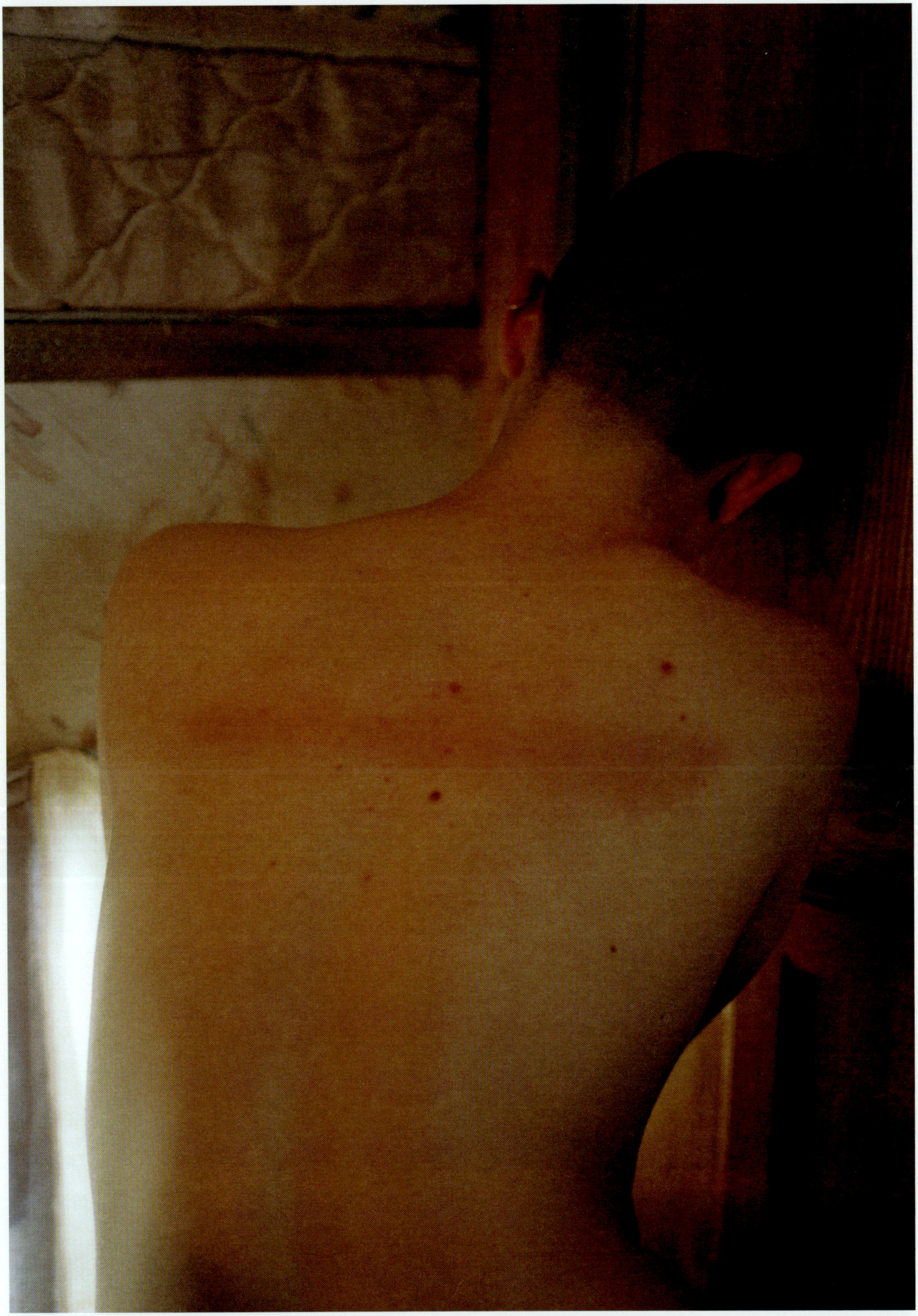

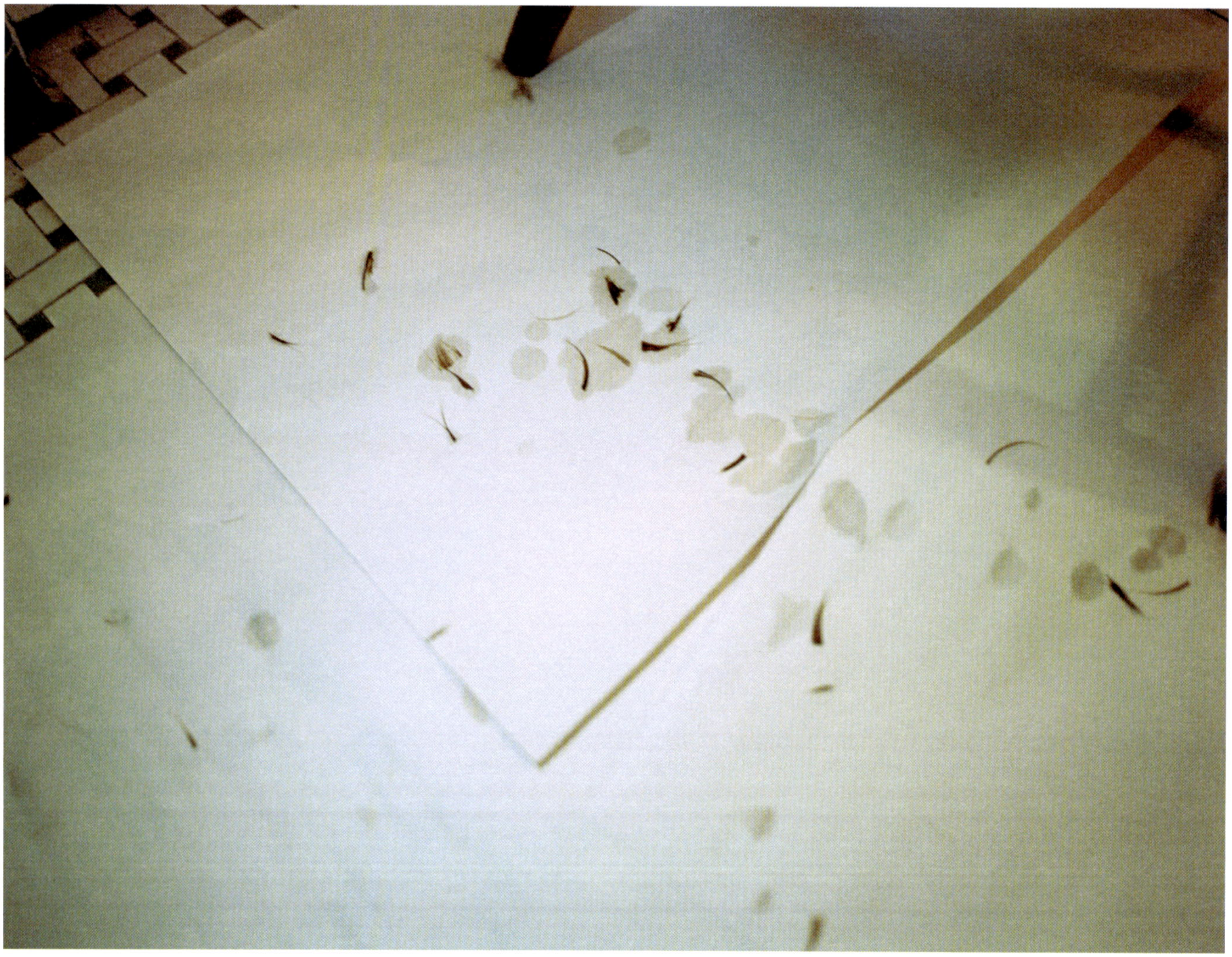

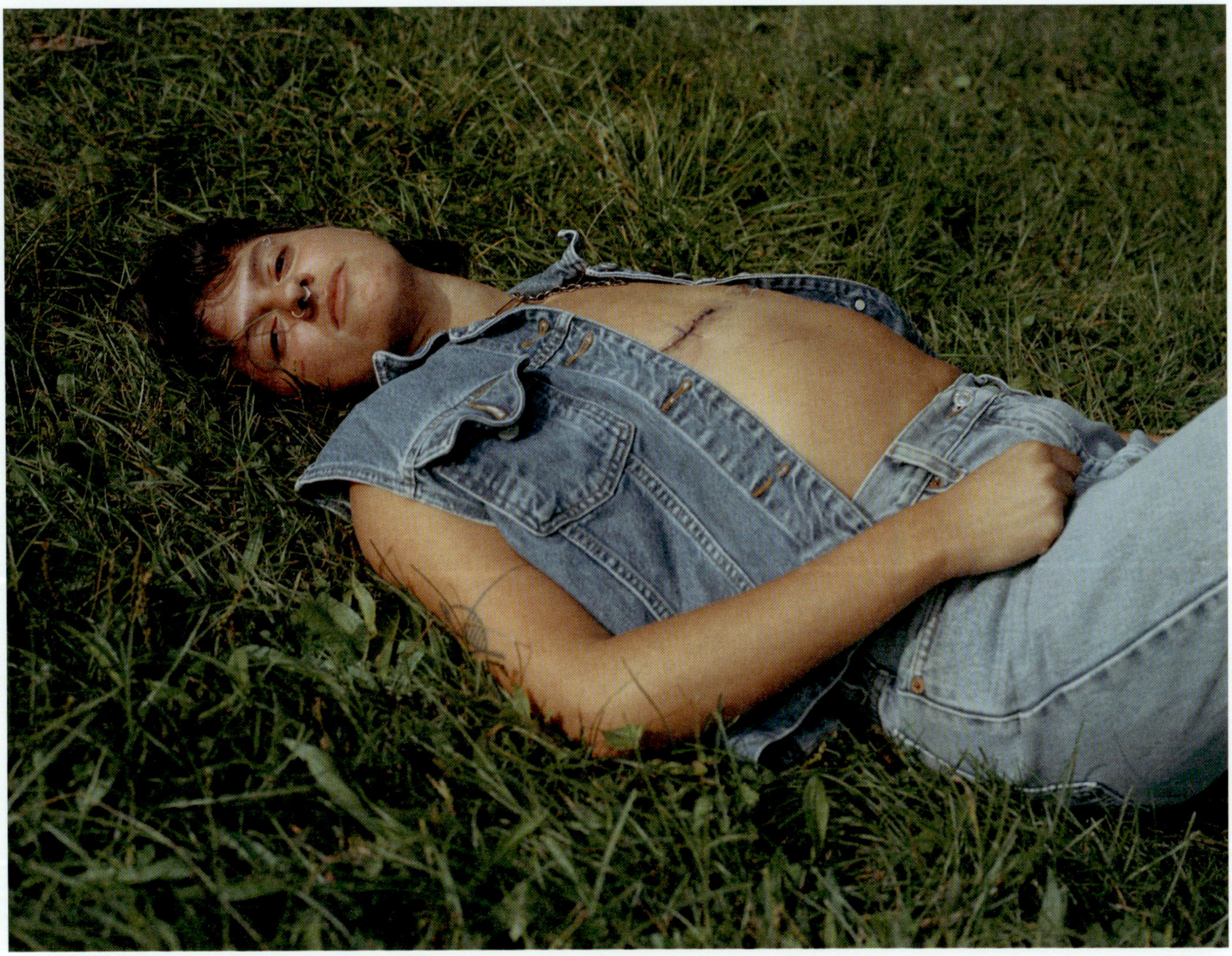

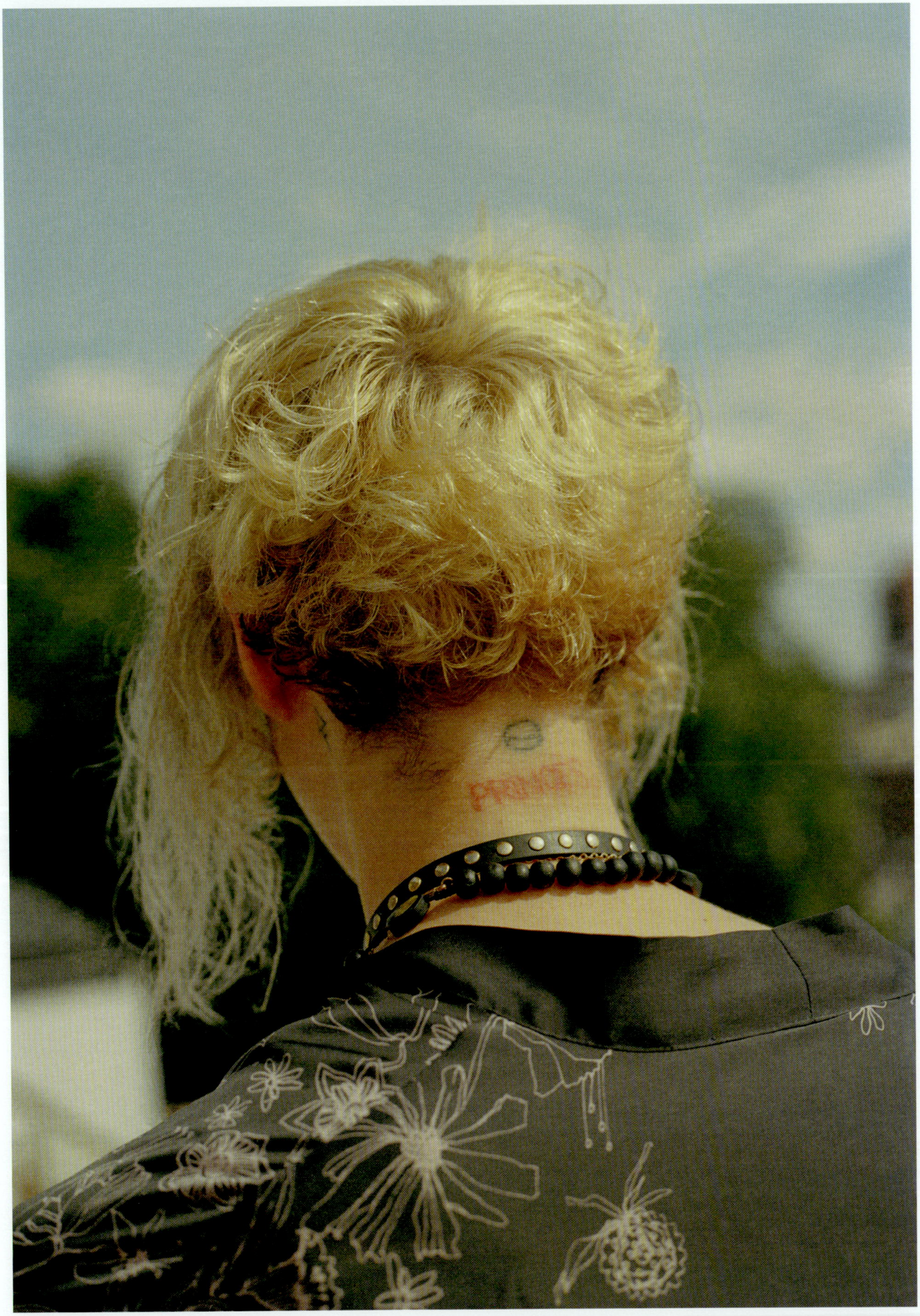

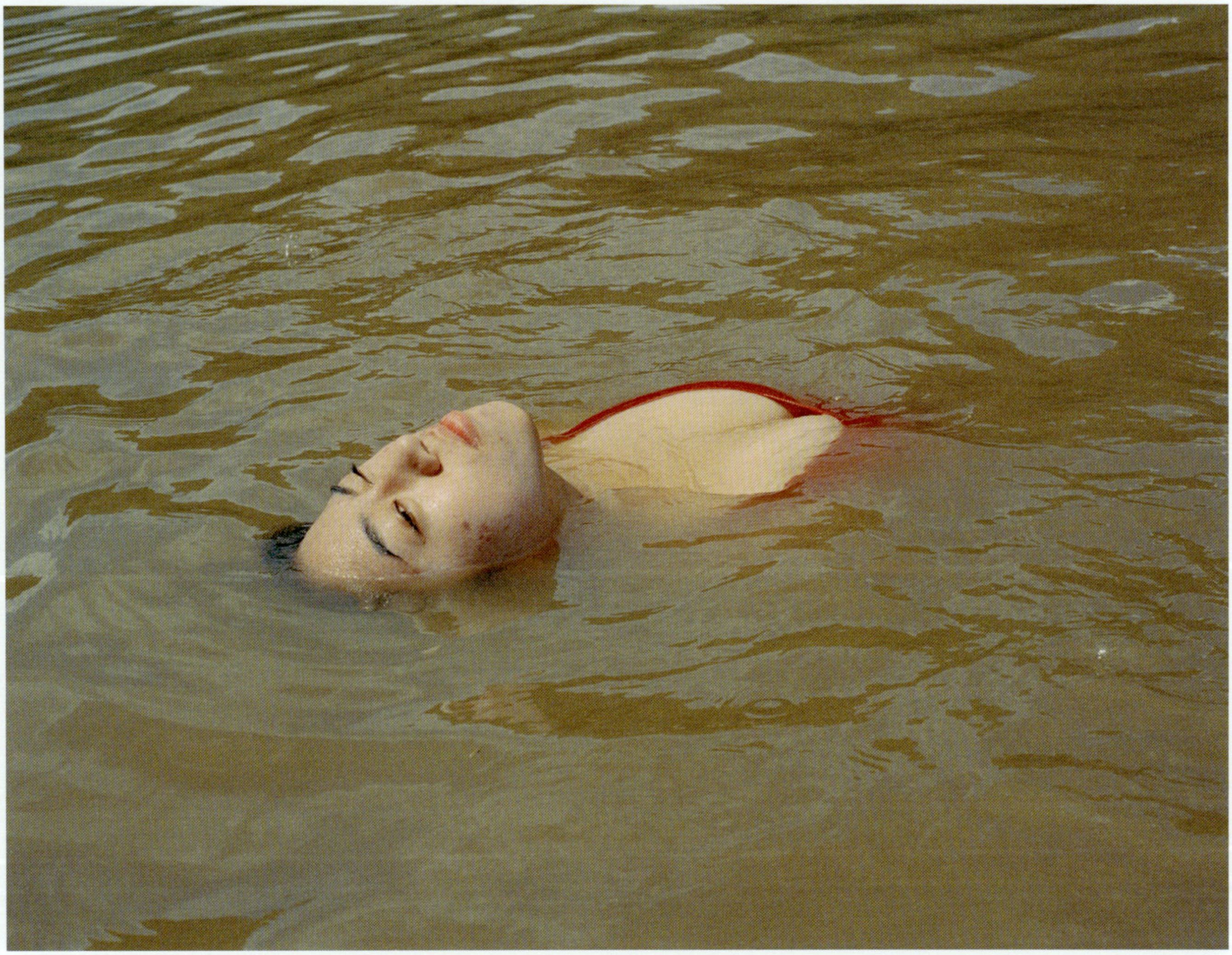

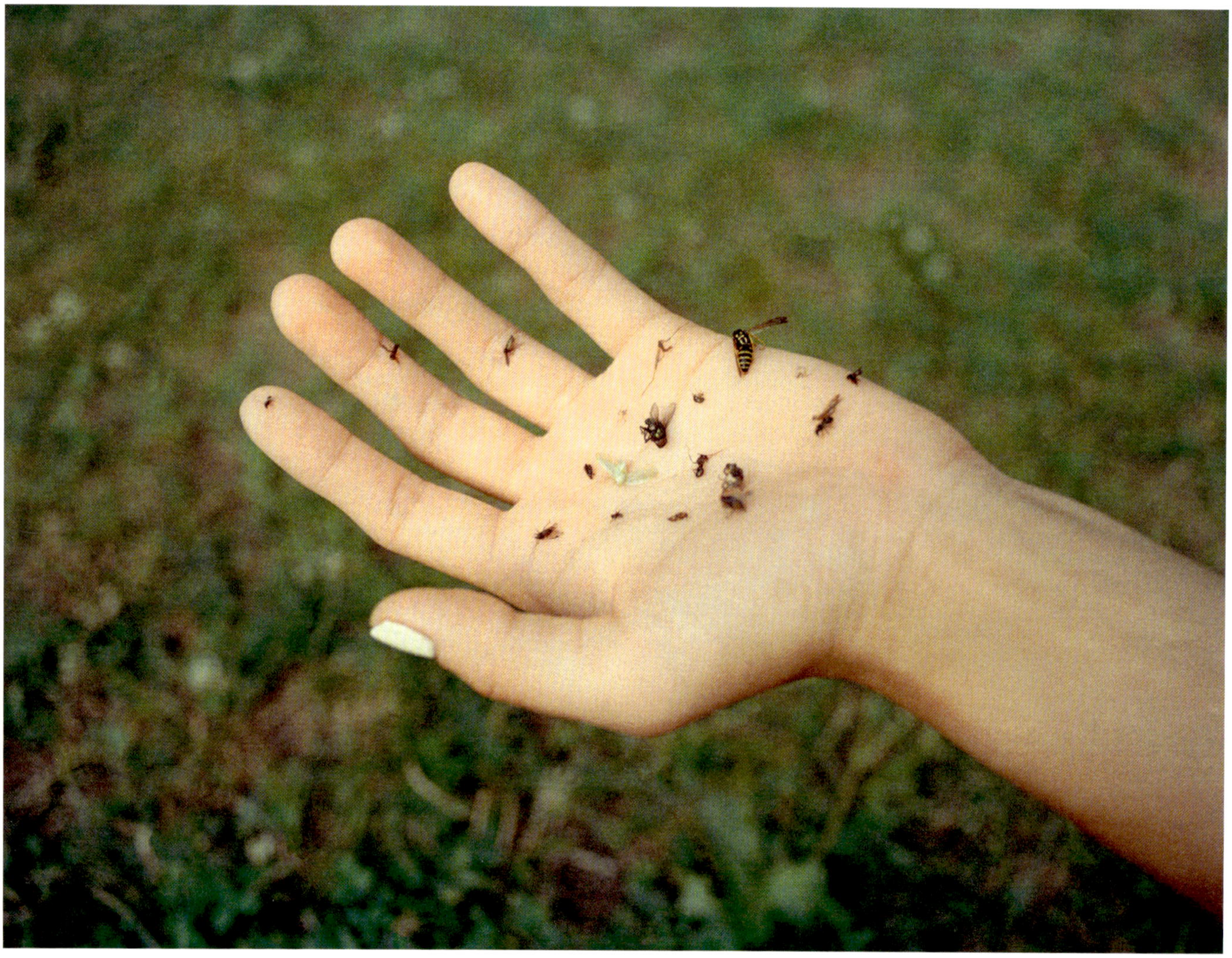

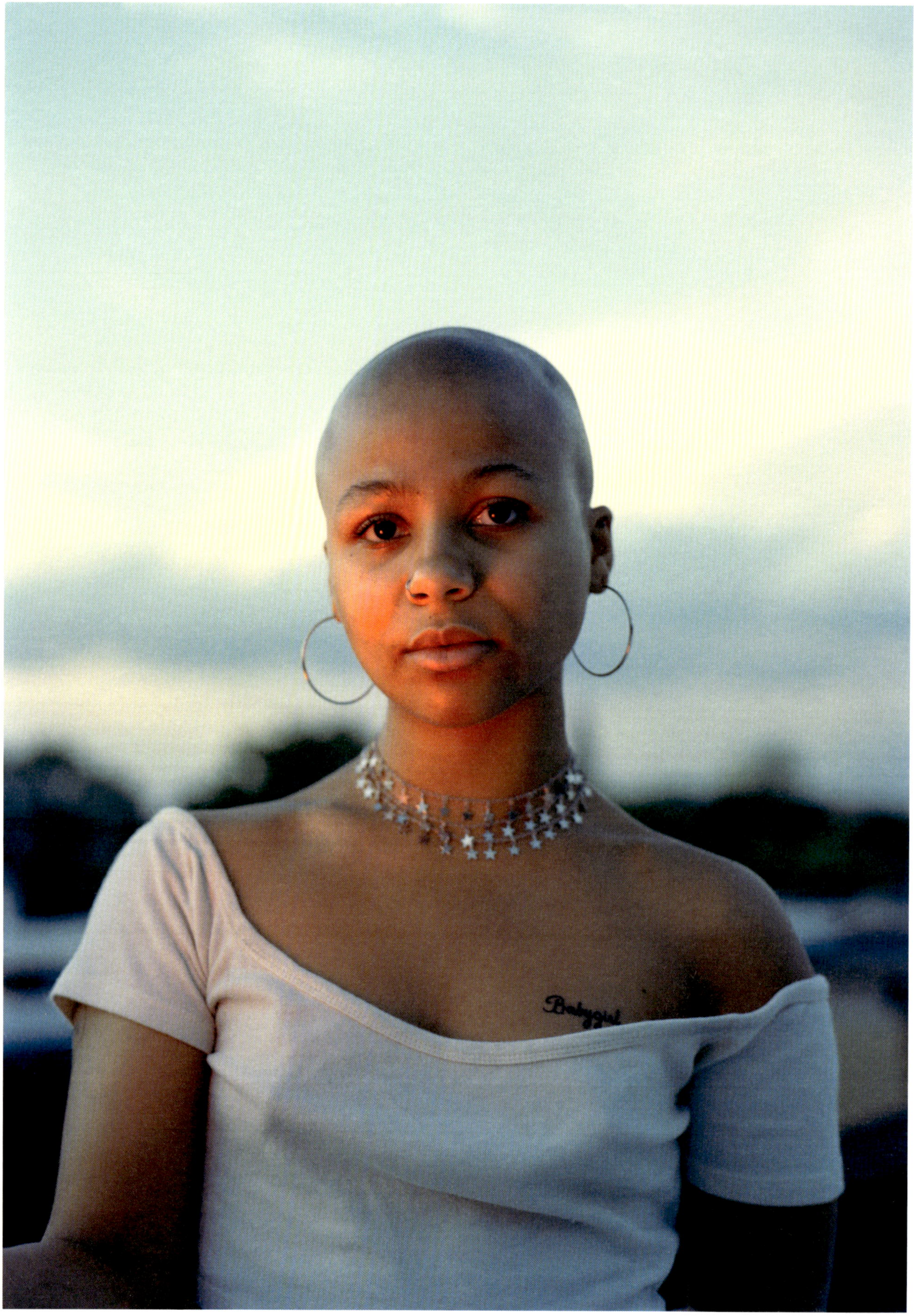
Babygirl

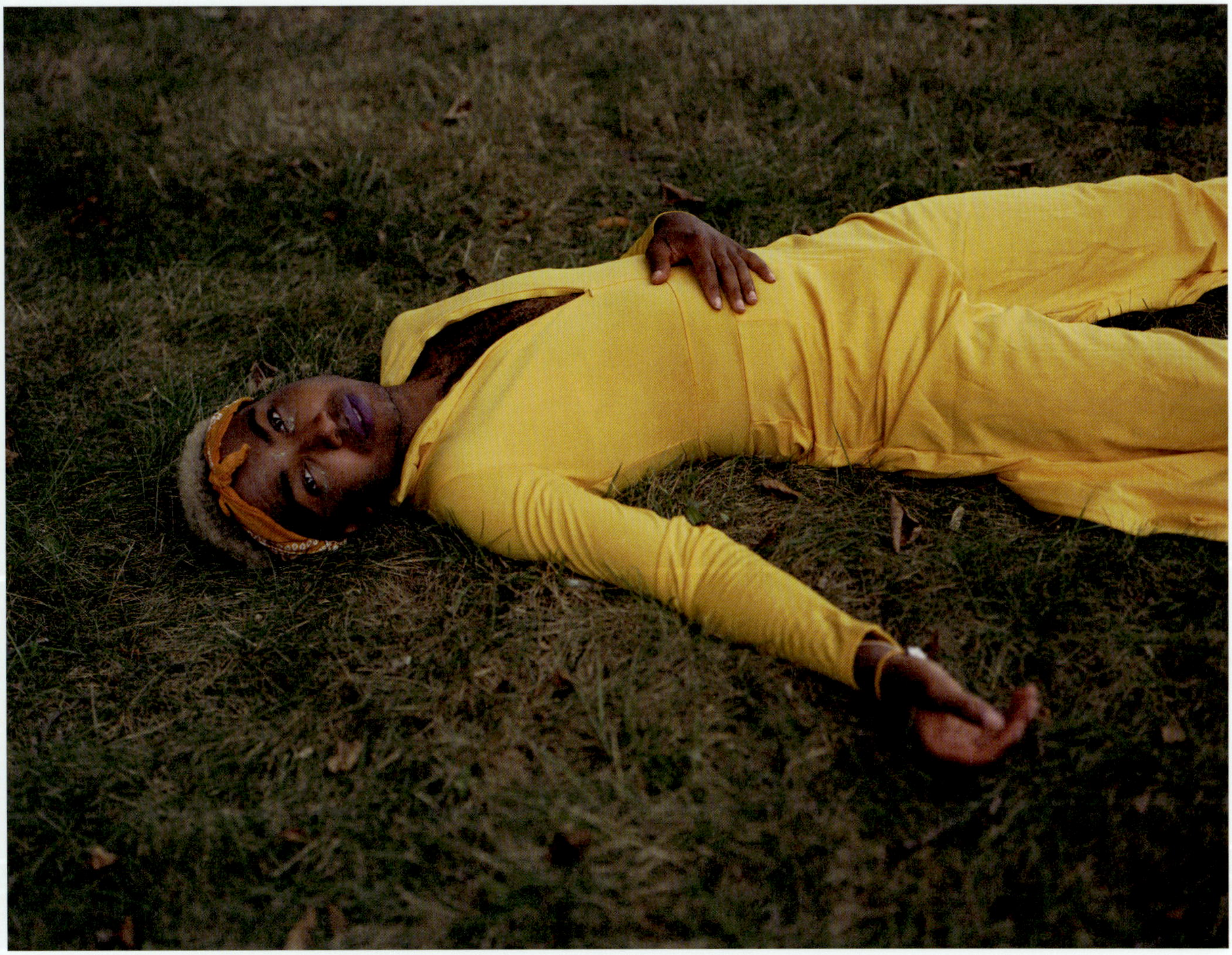

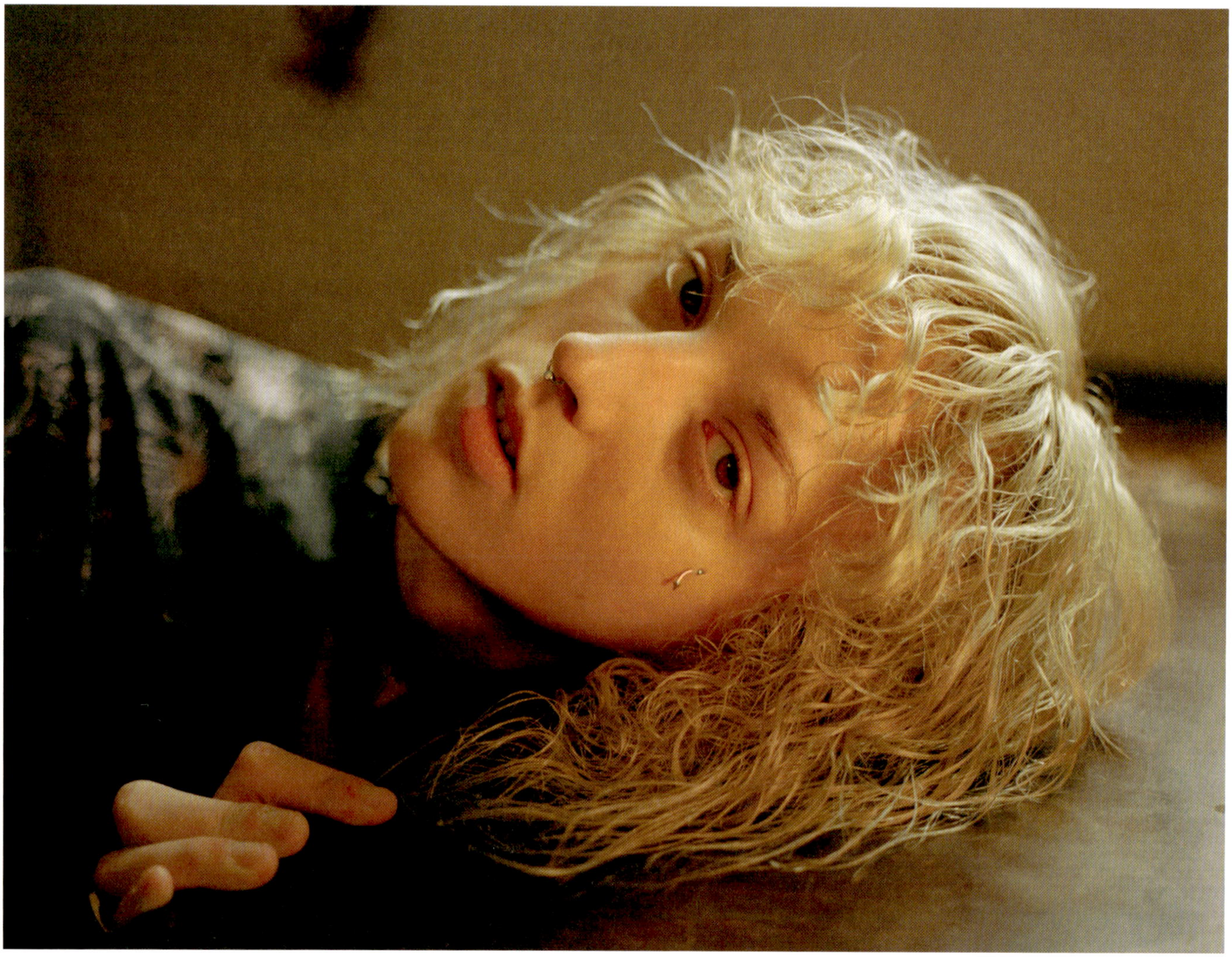

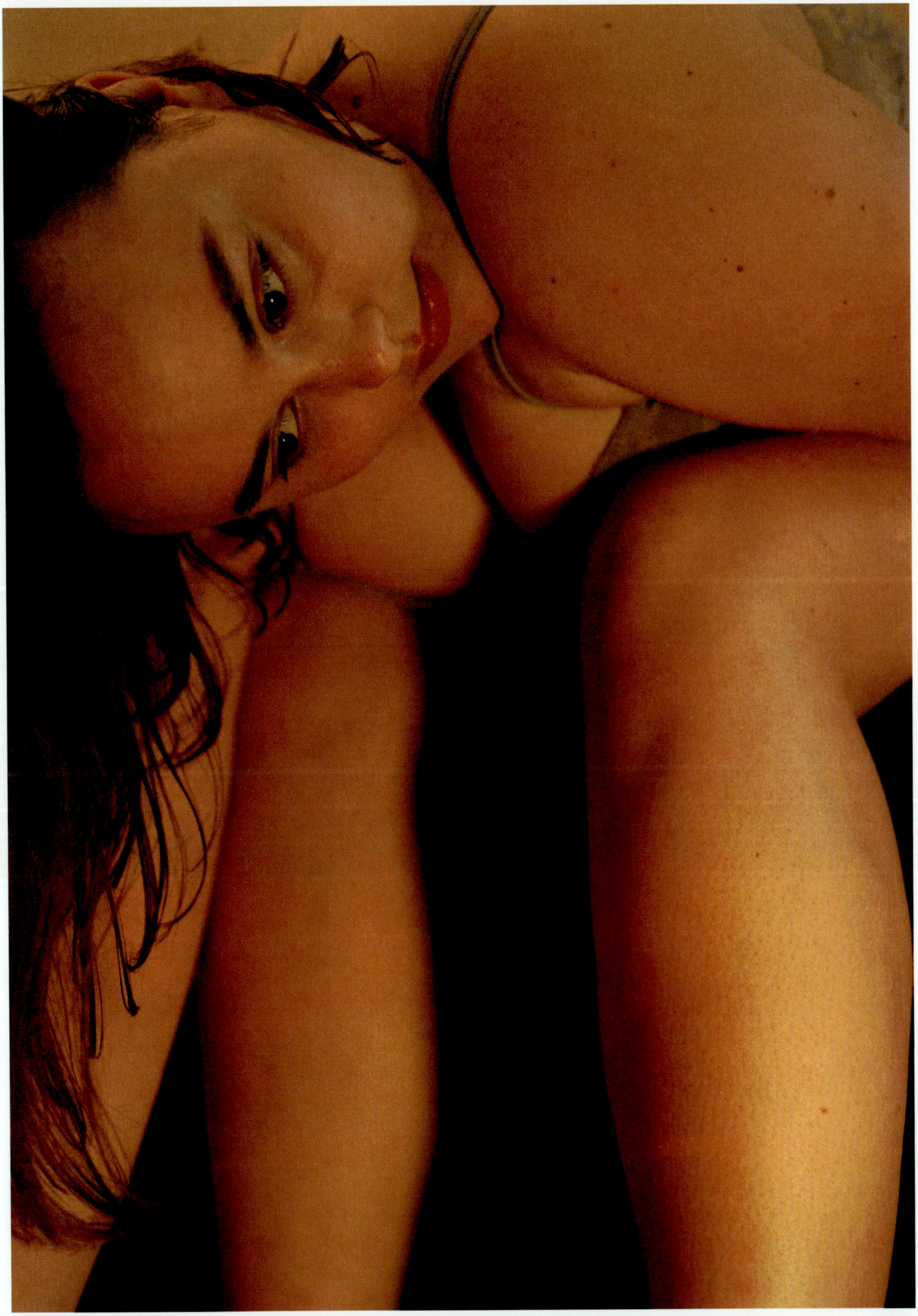

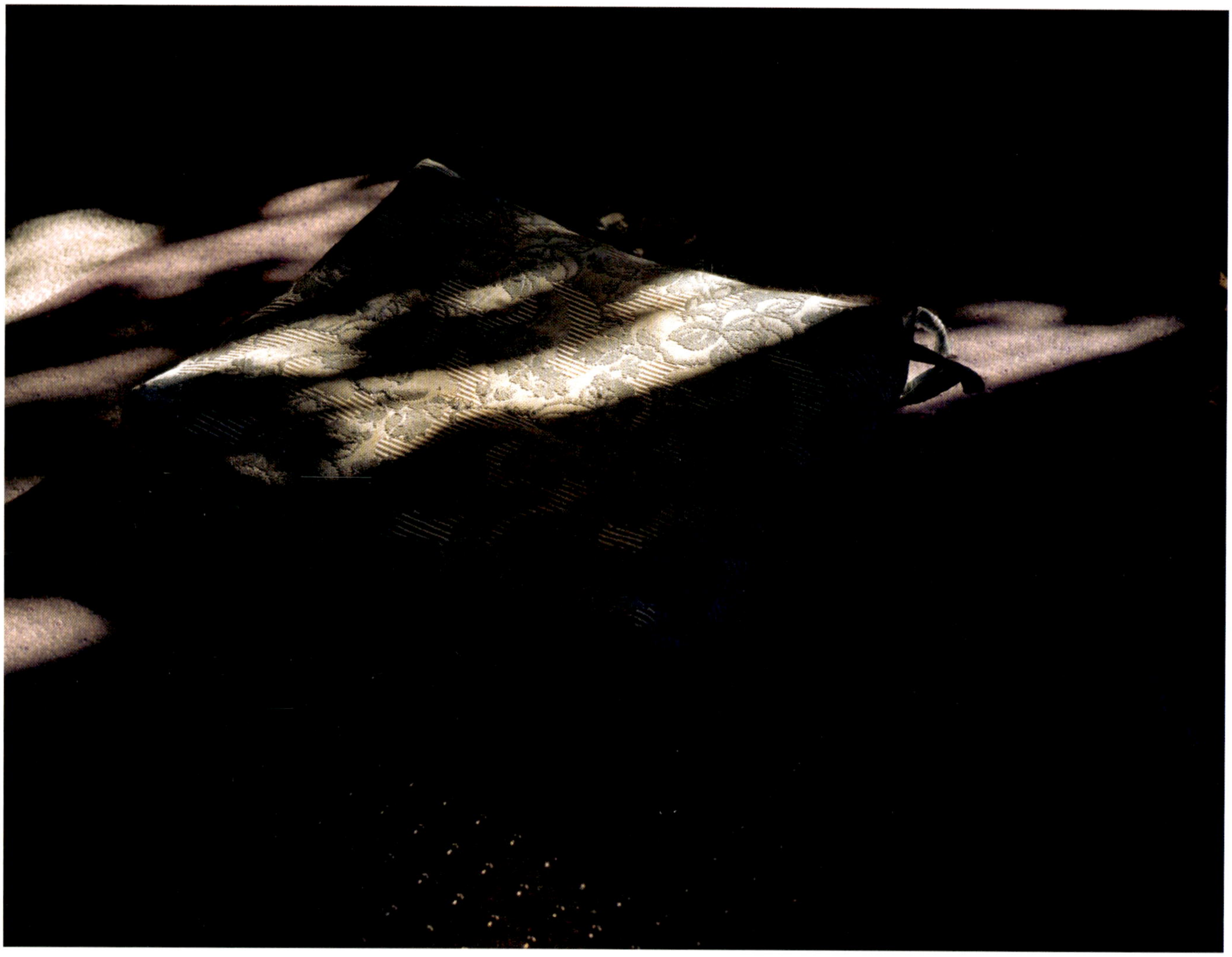

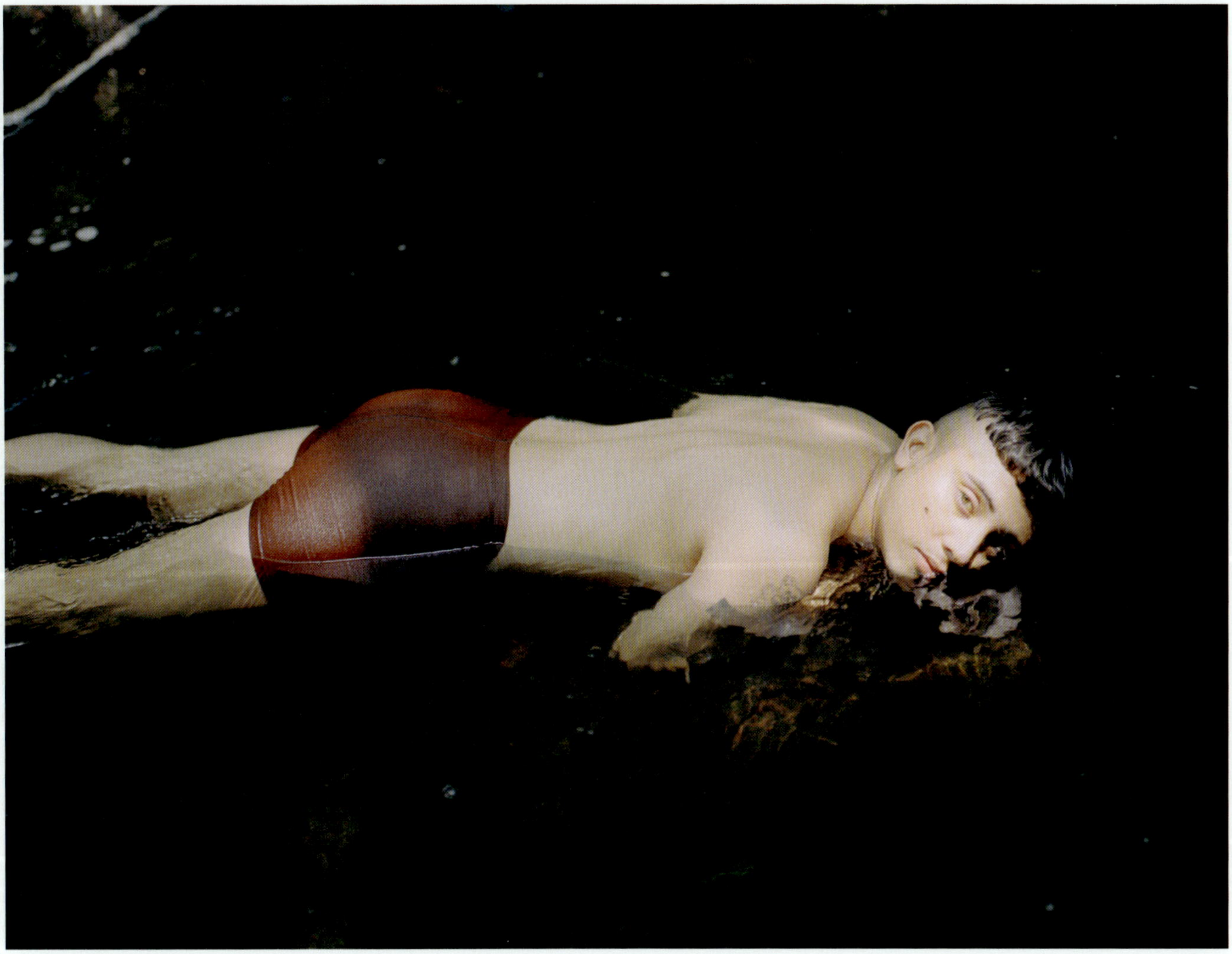

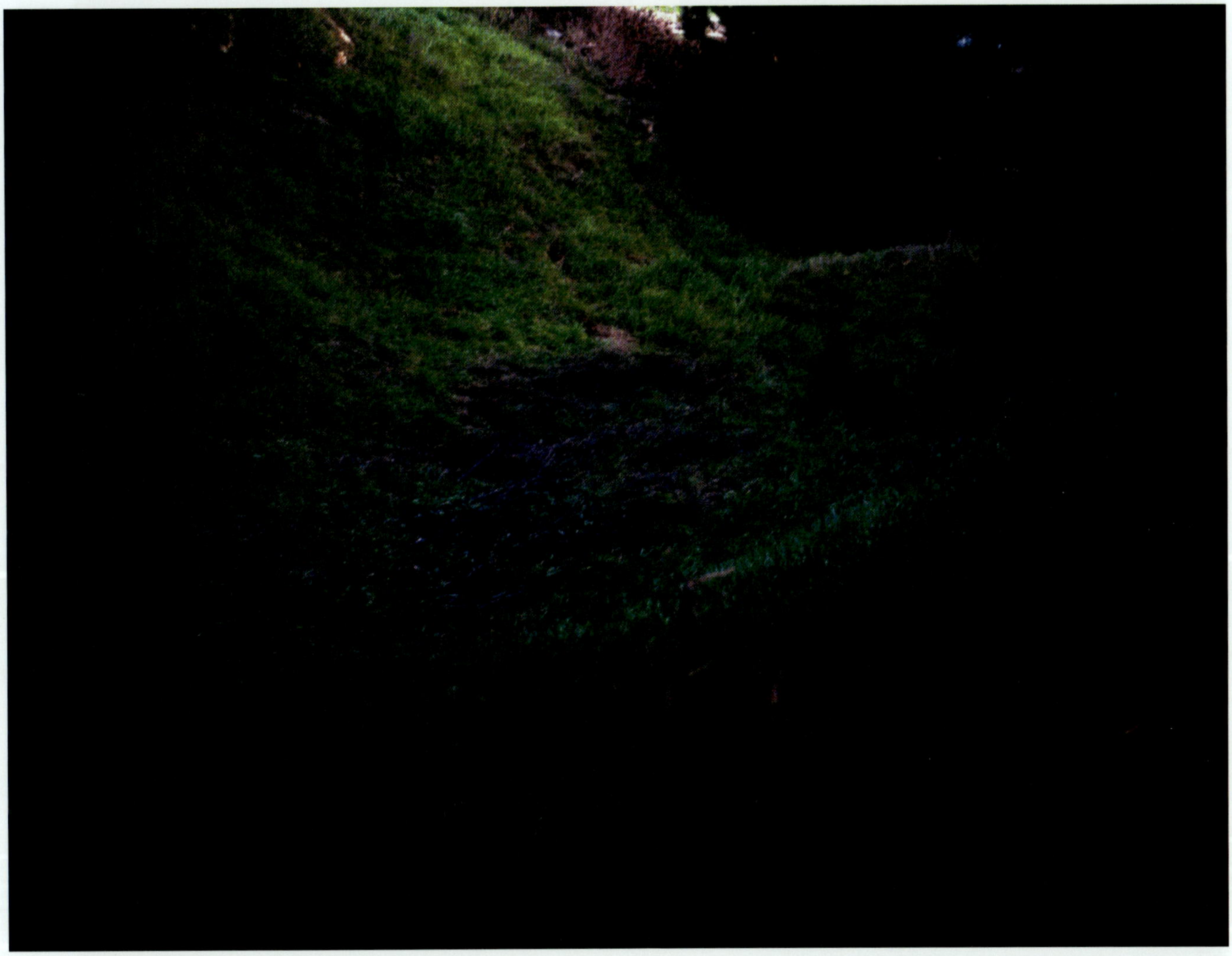

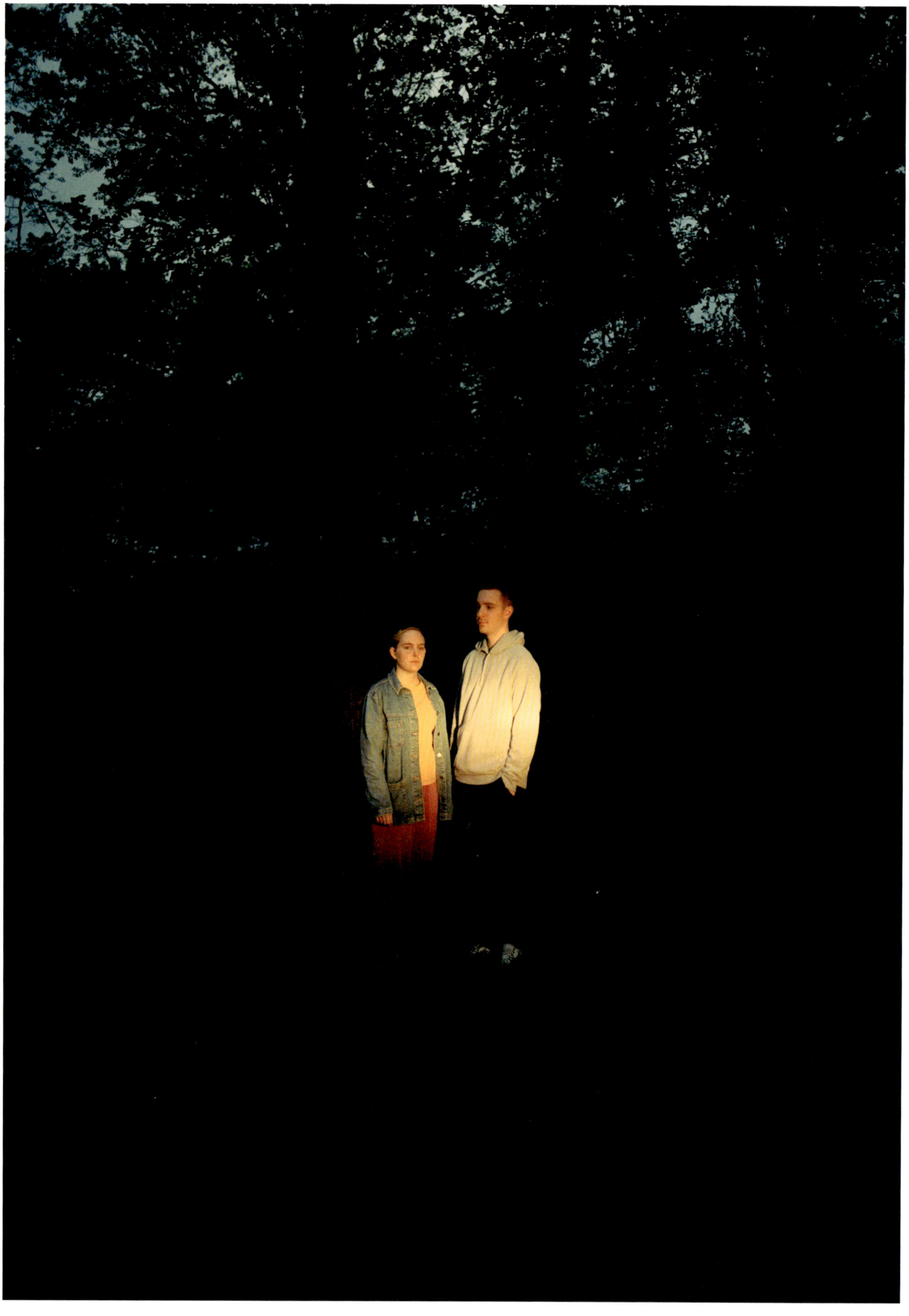

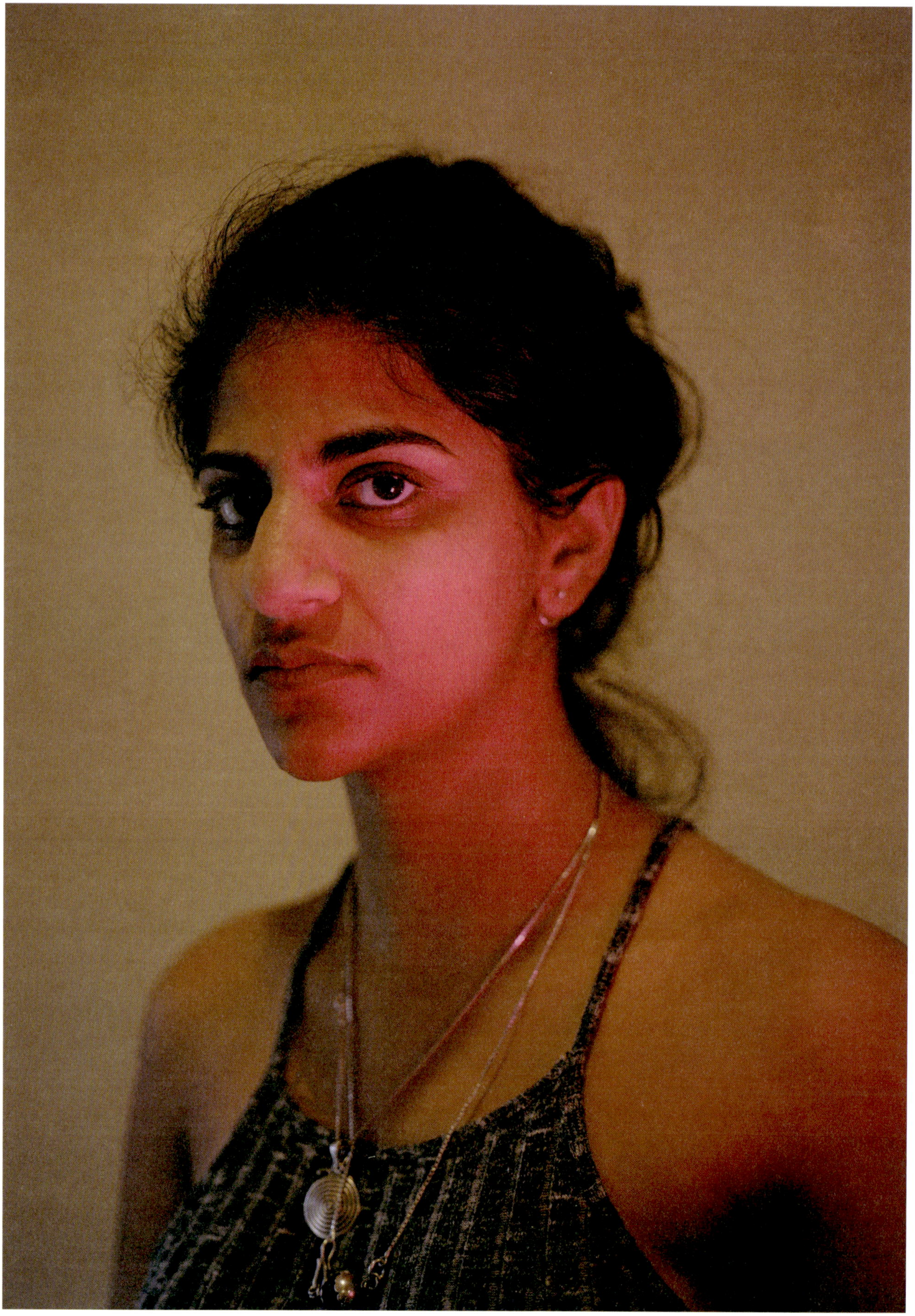

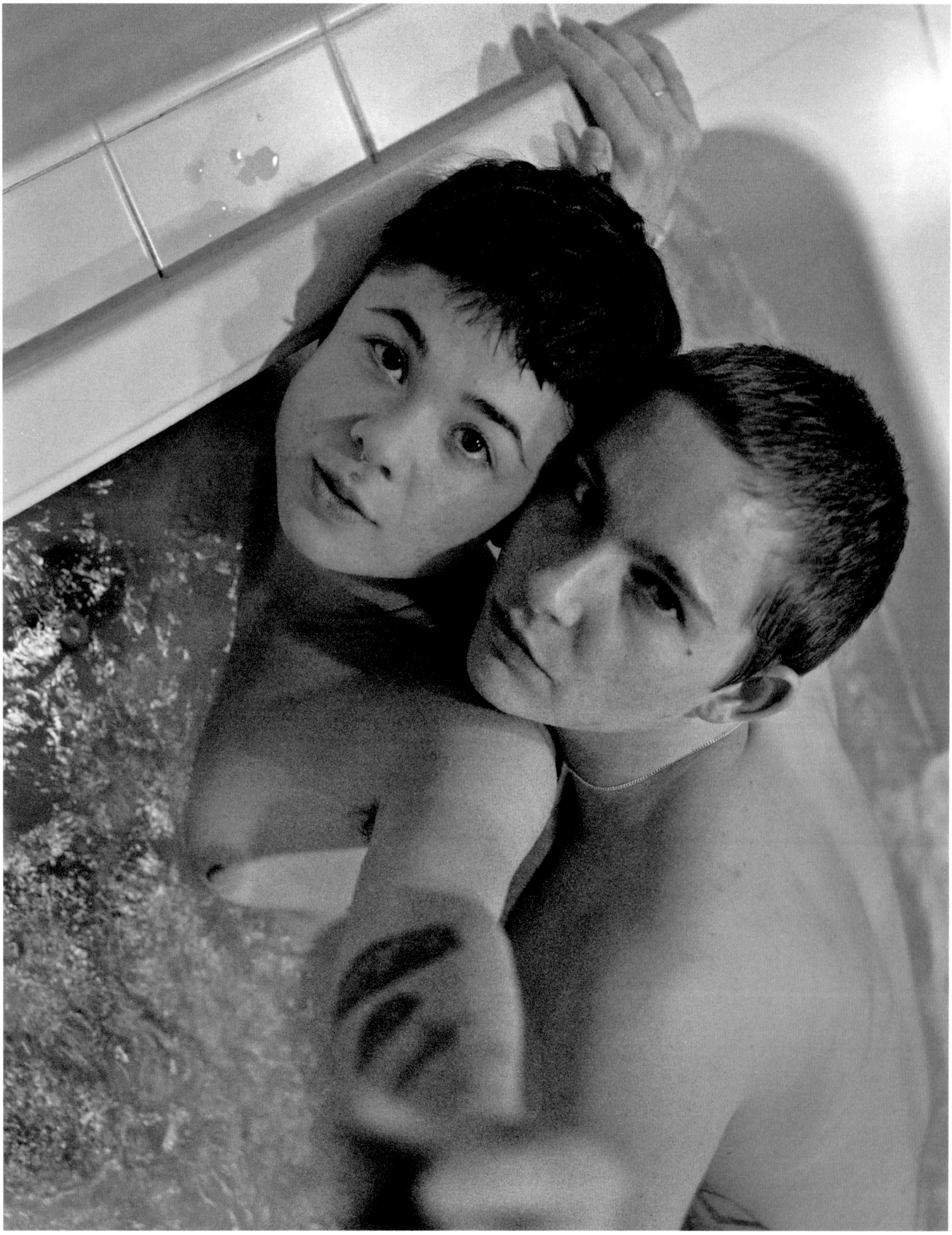

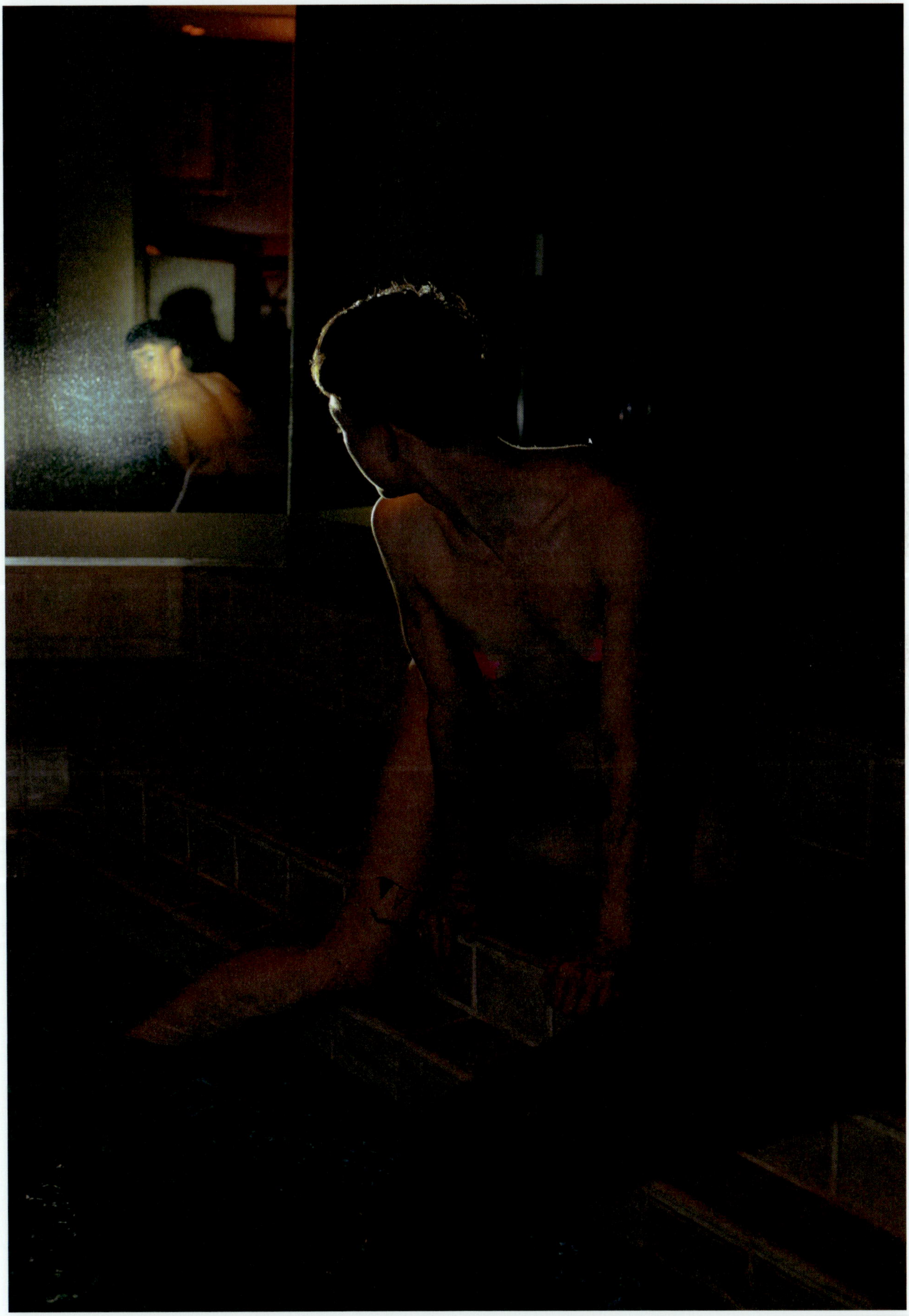

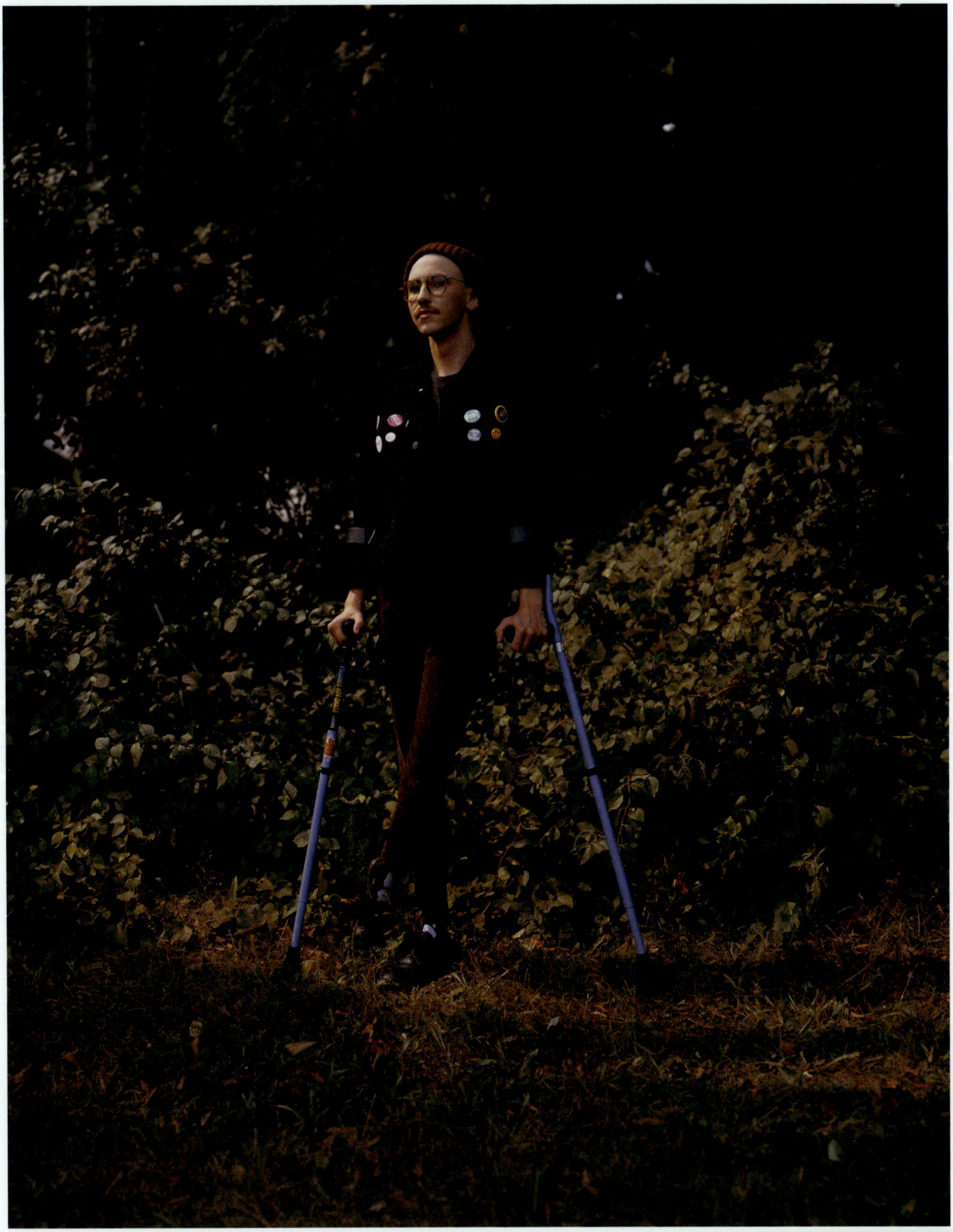

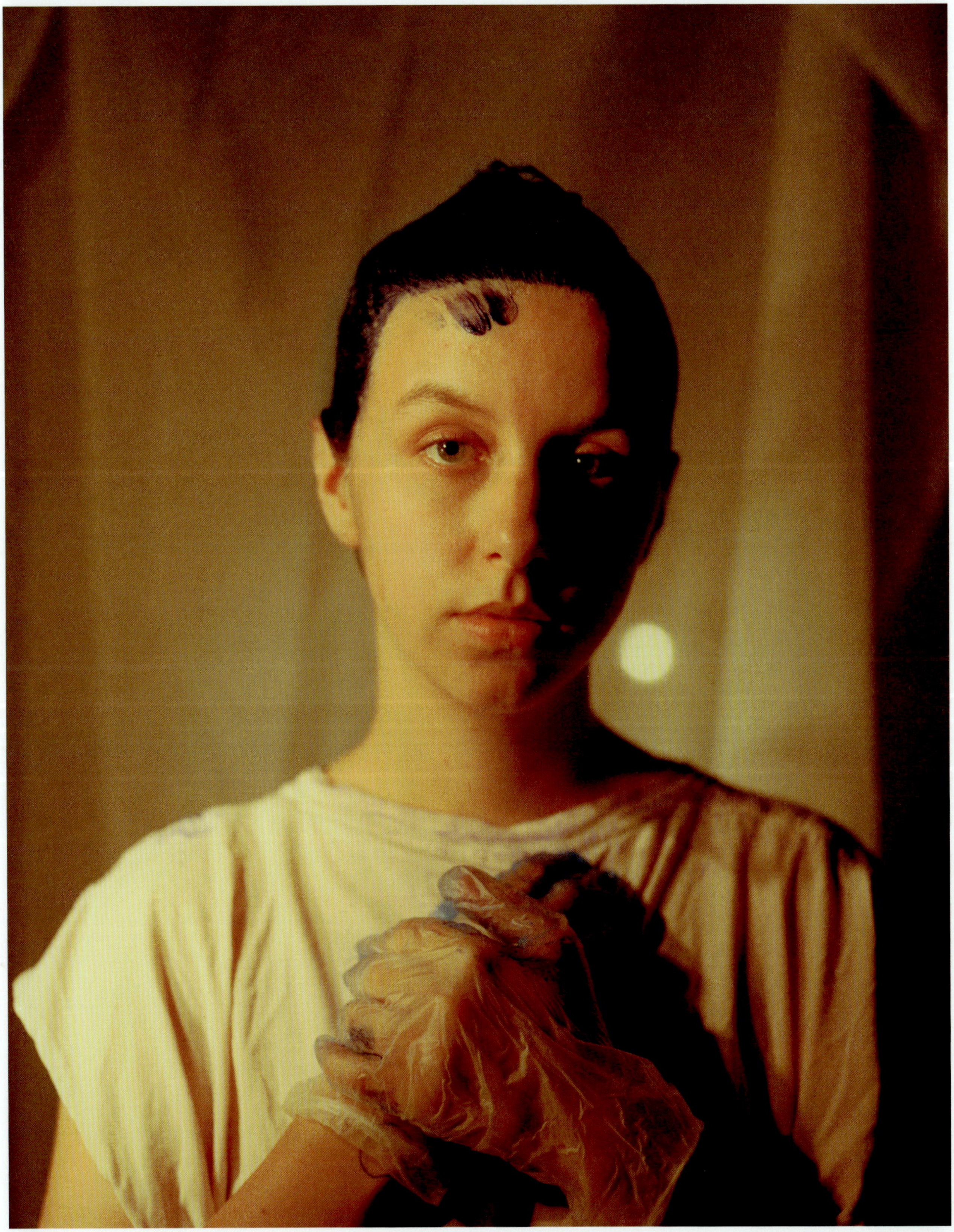

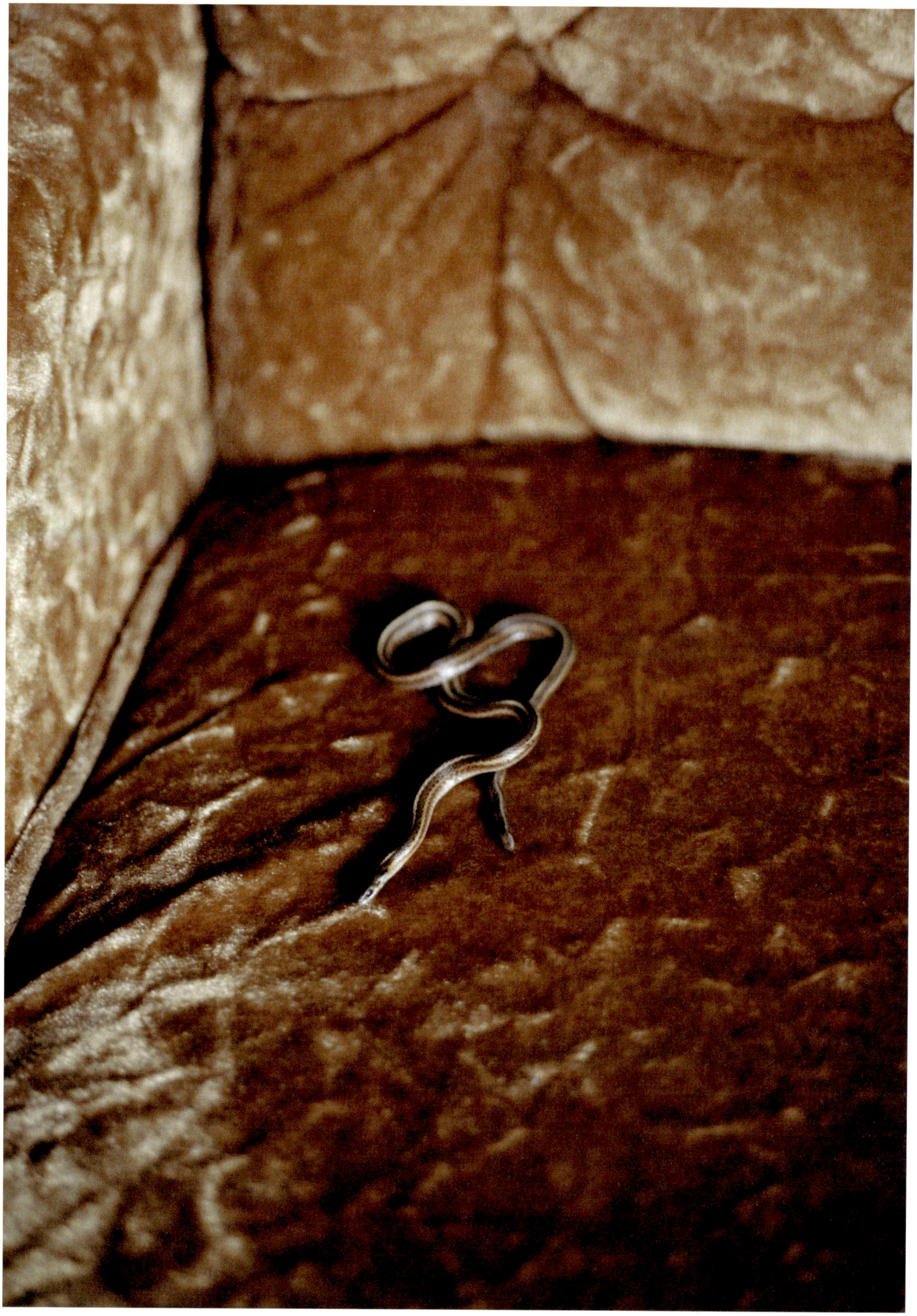

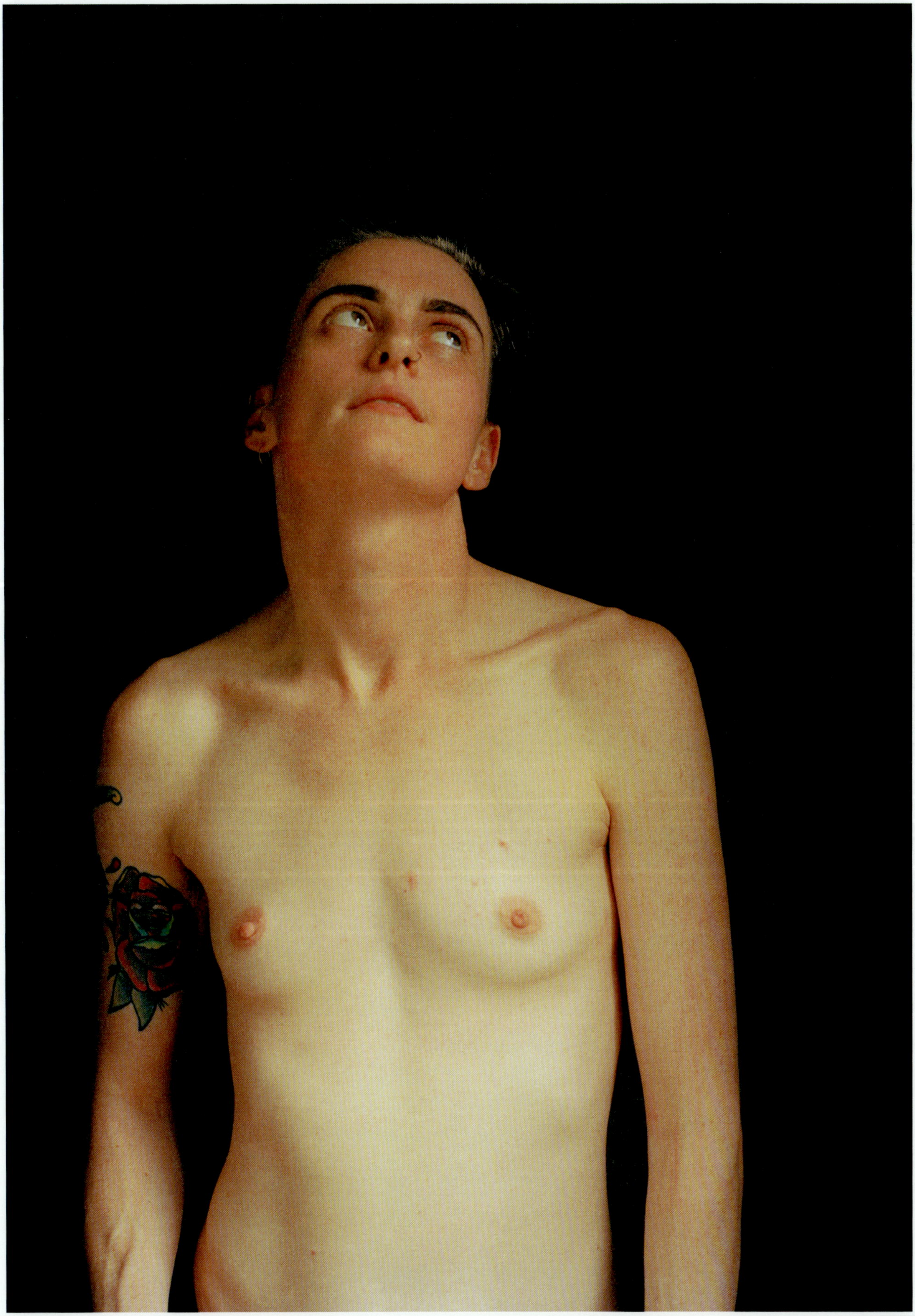

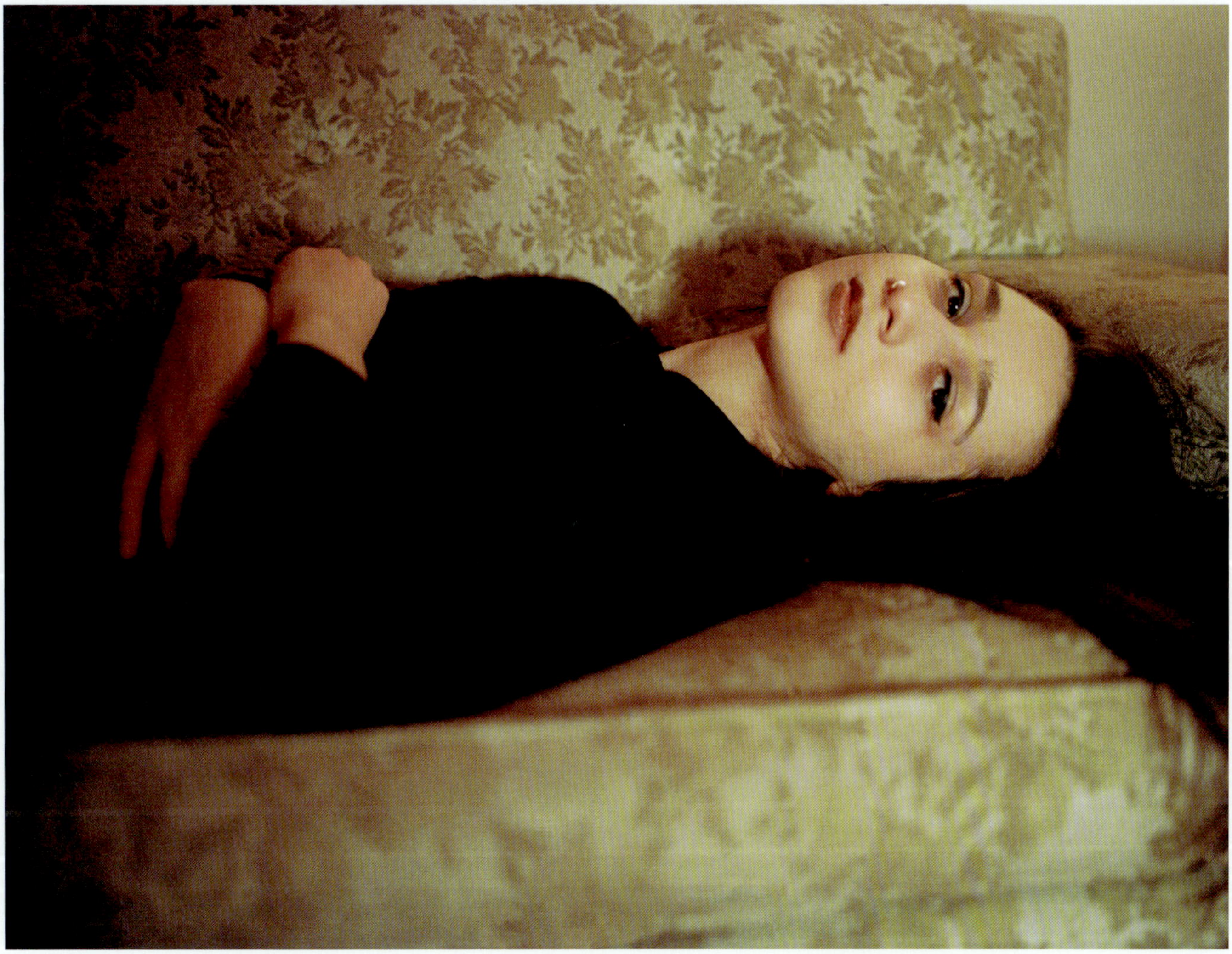

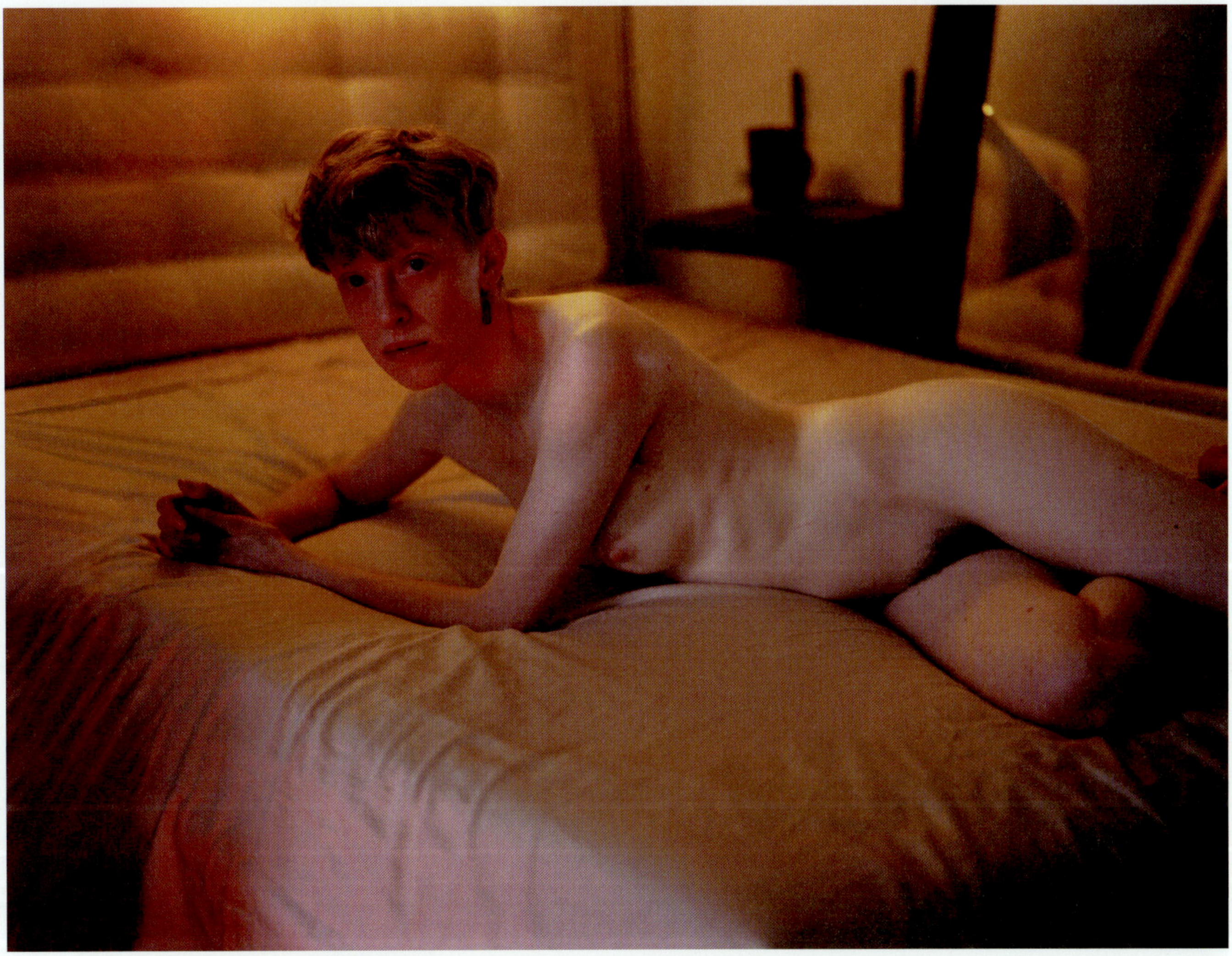

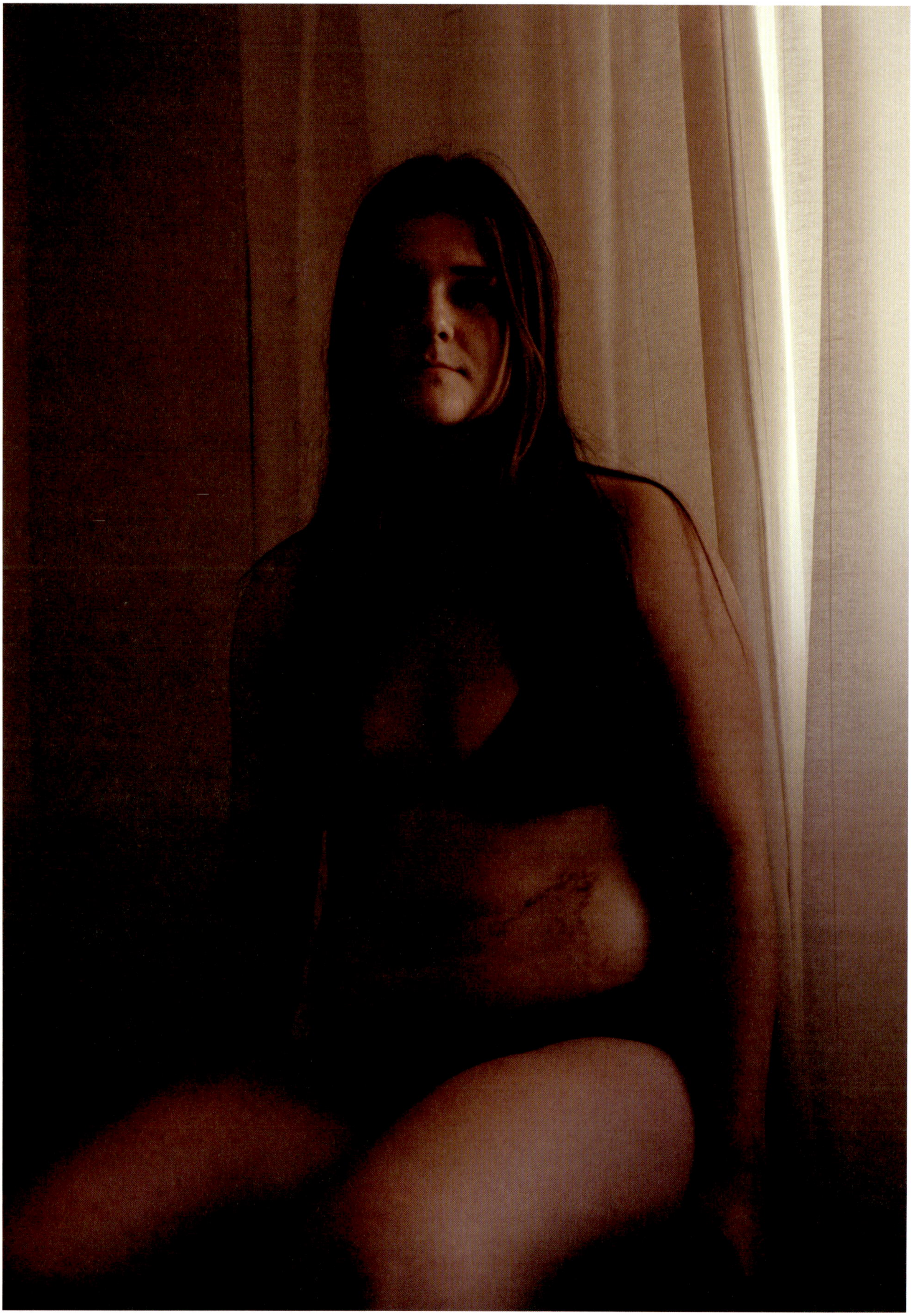

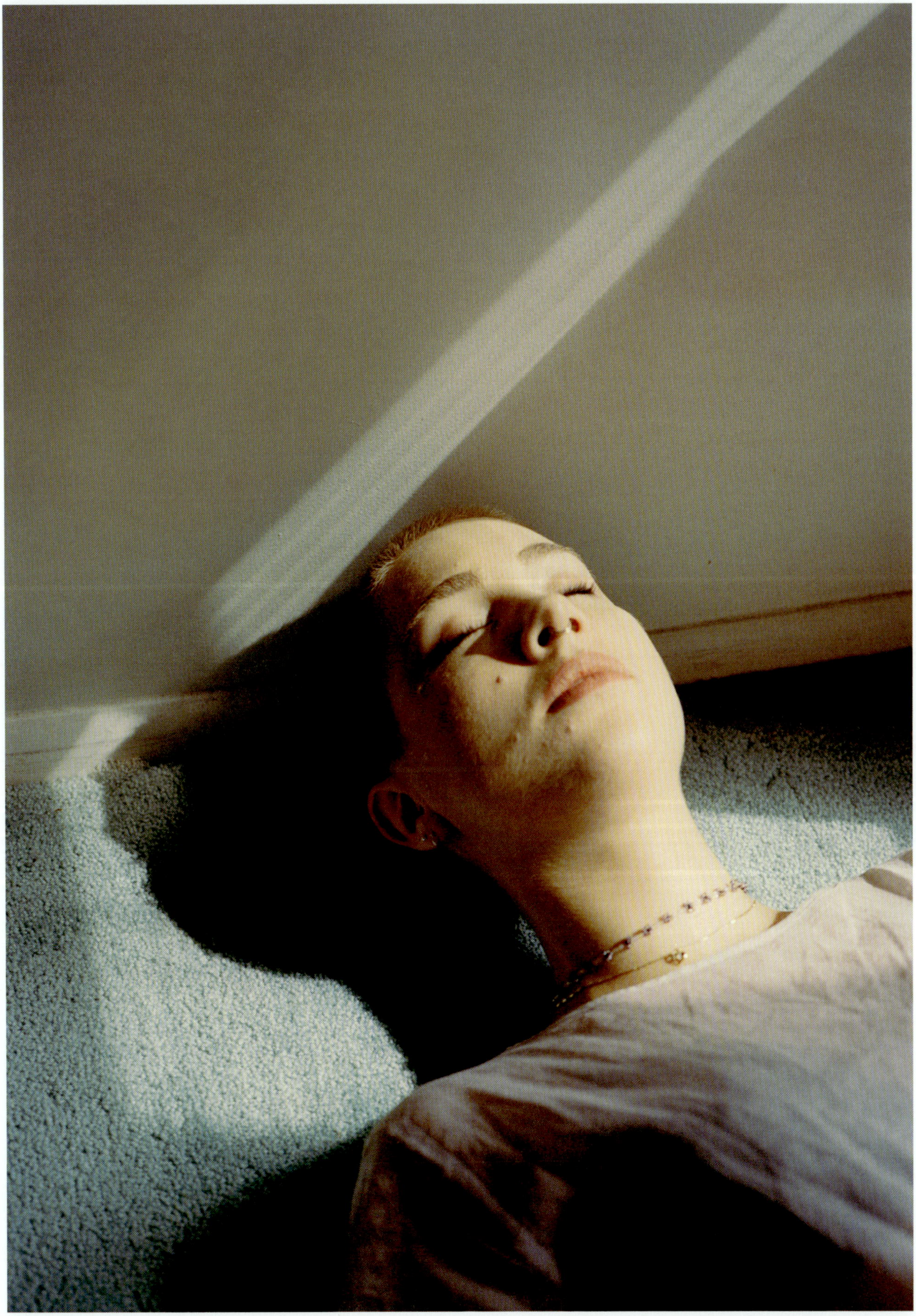

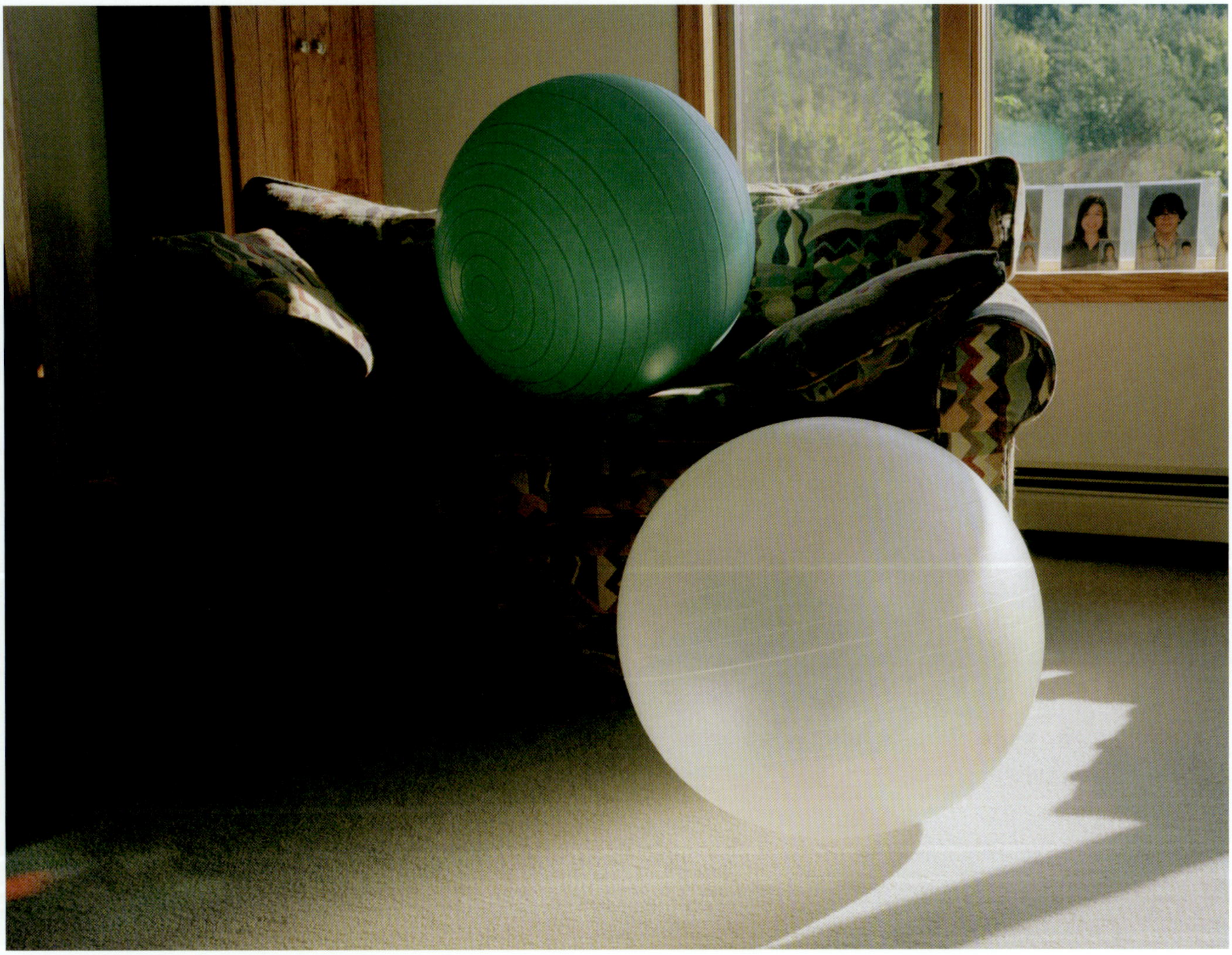

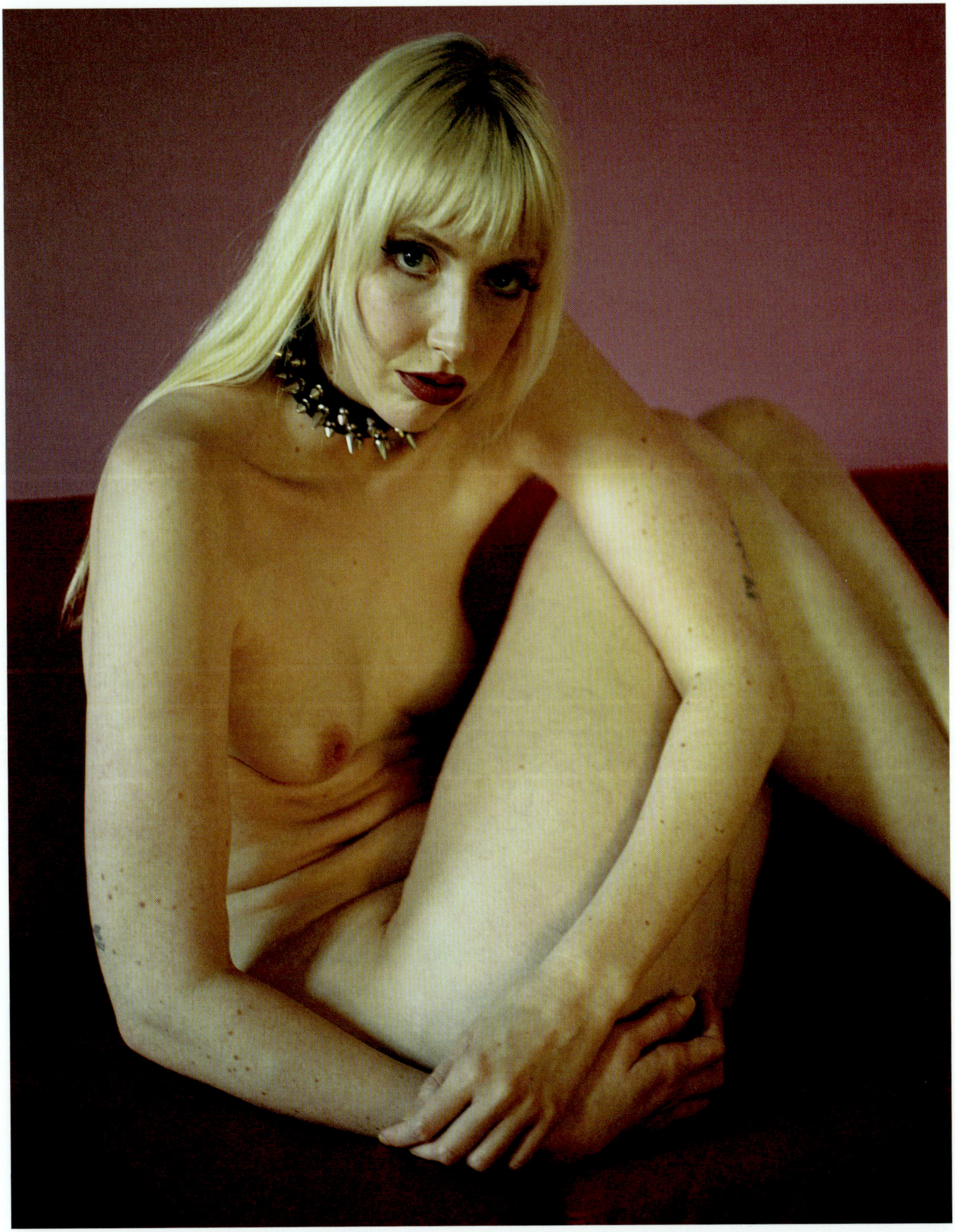

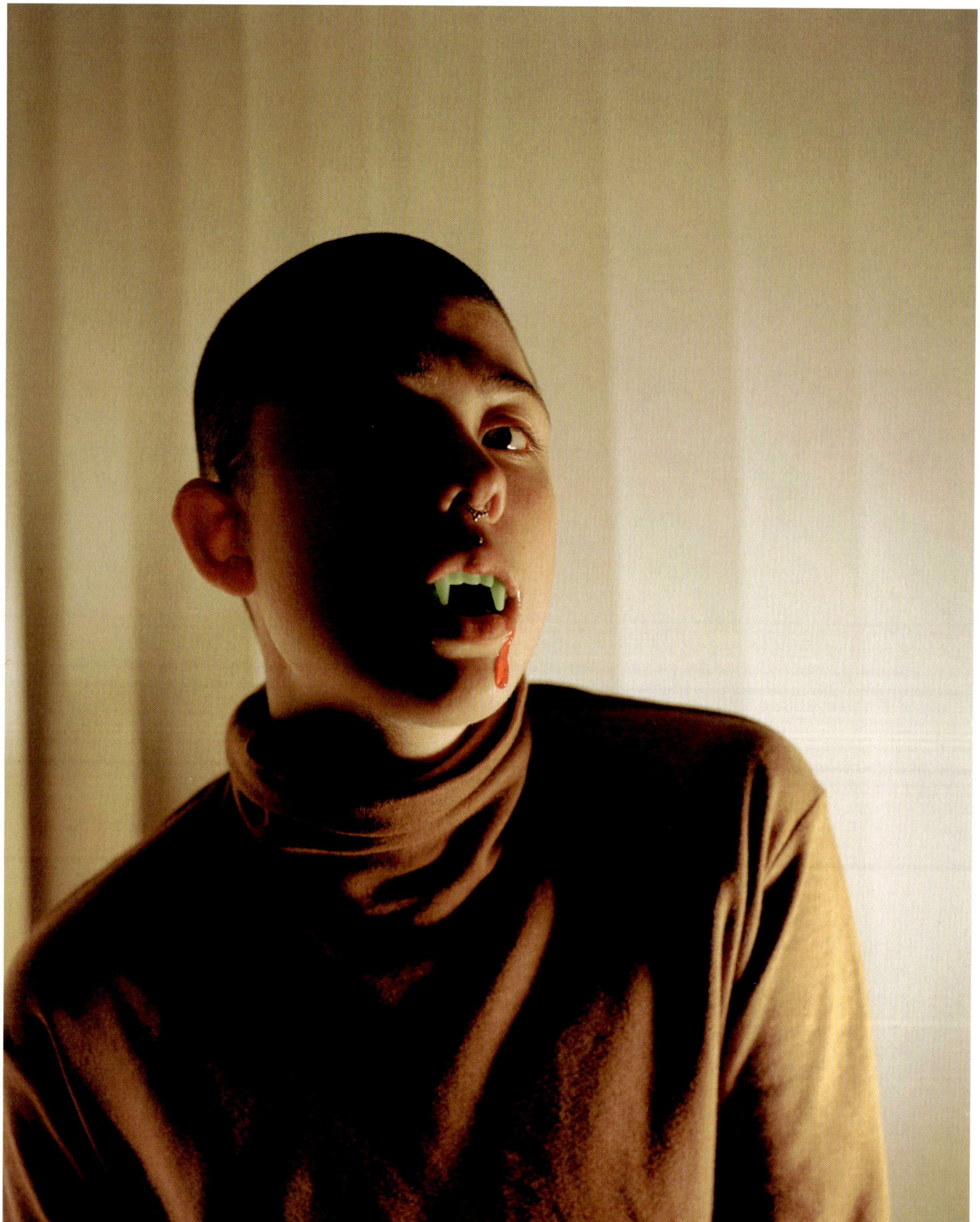

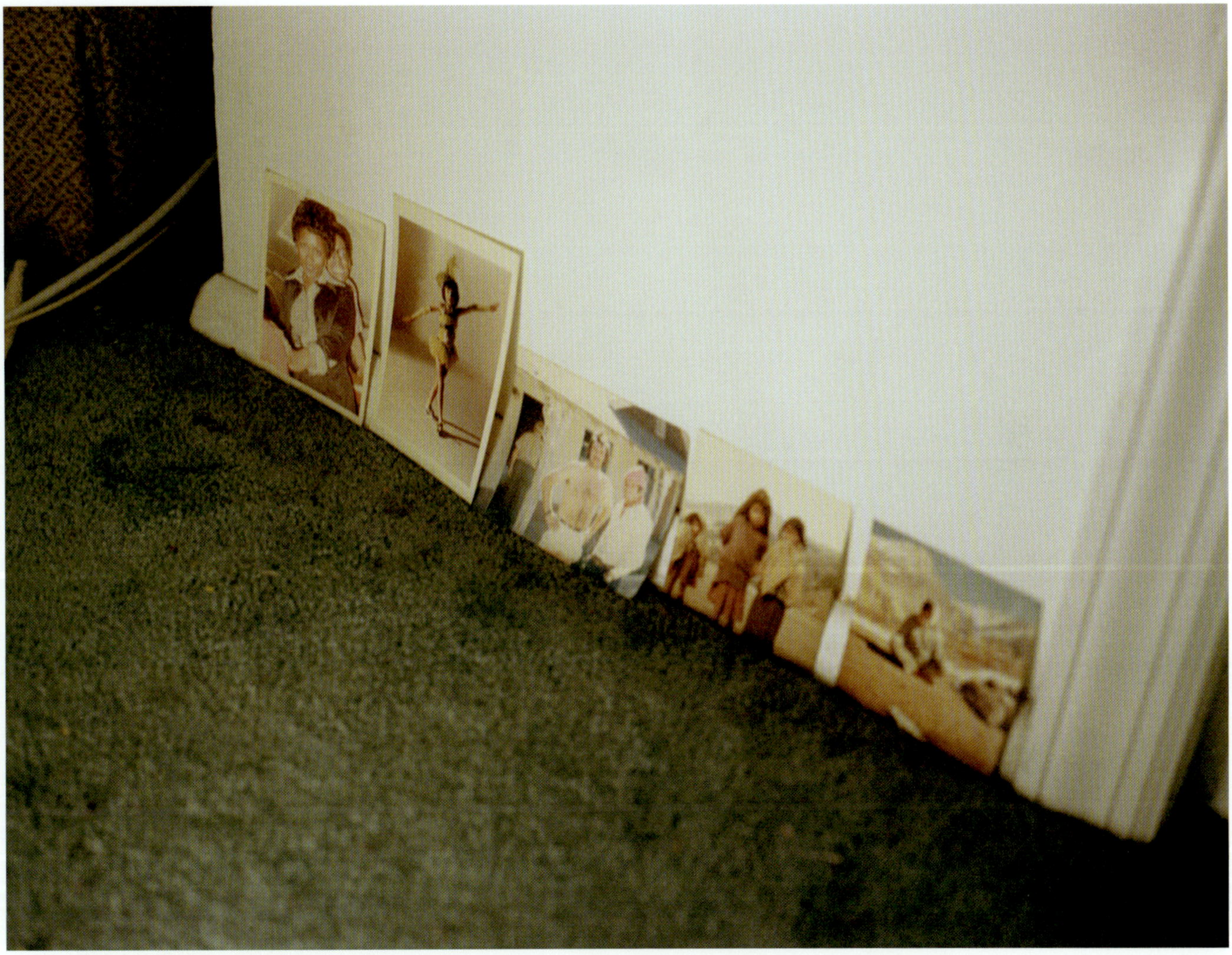

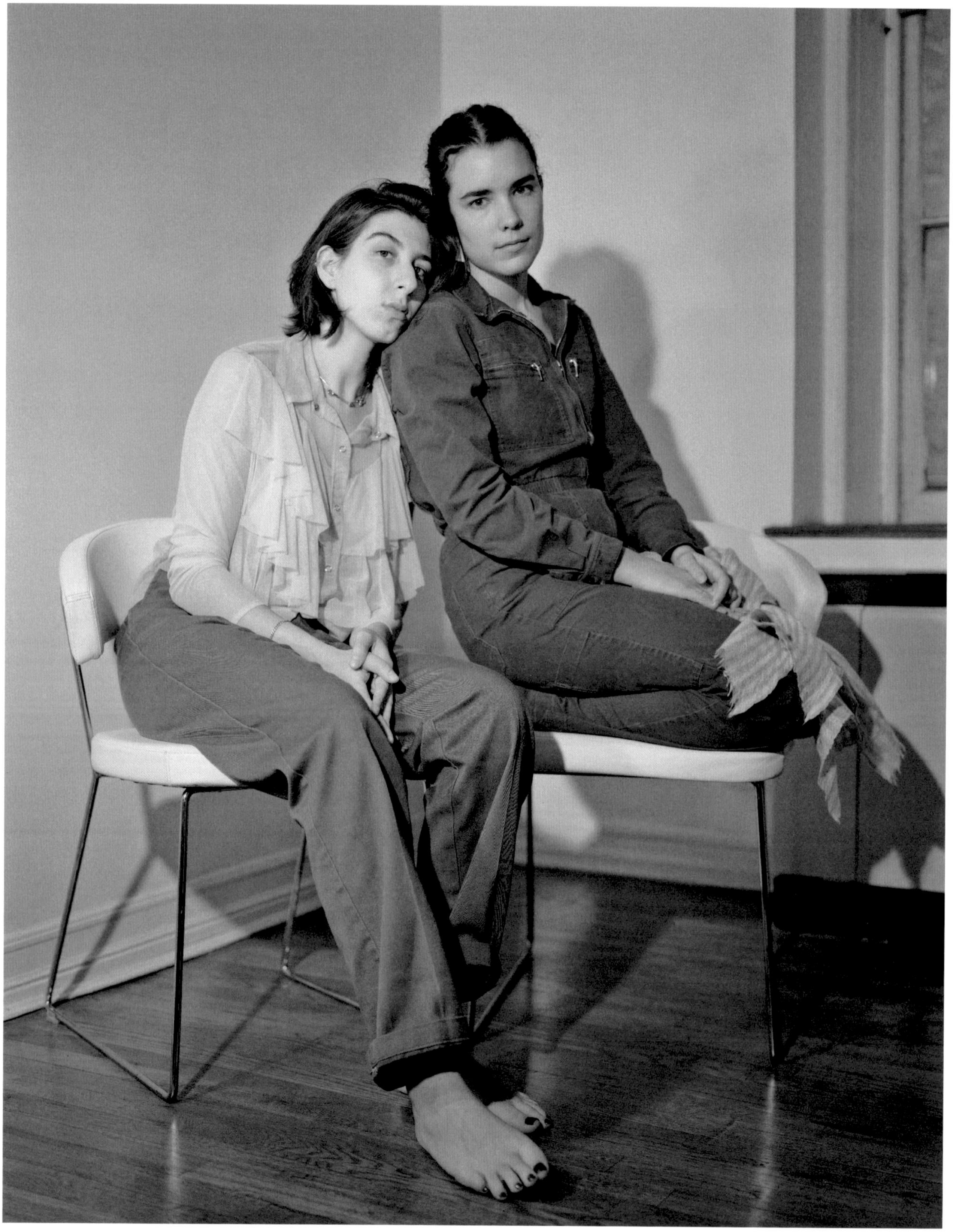

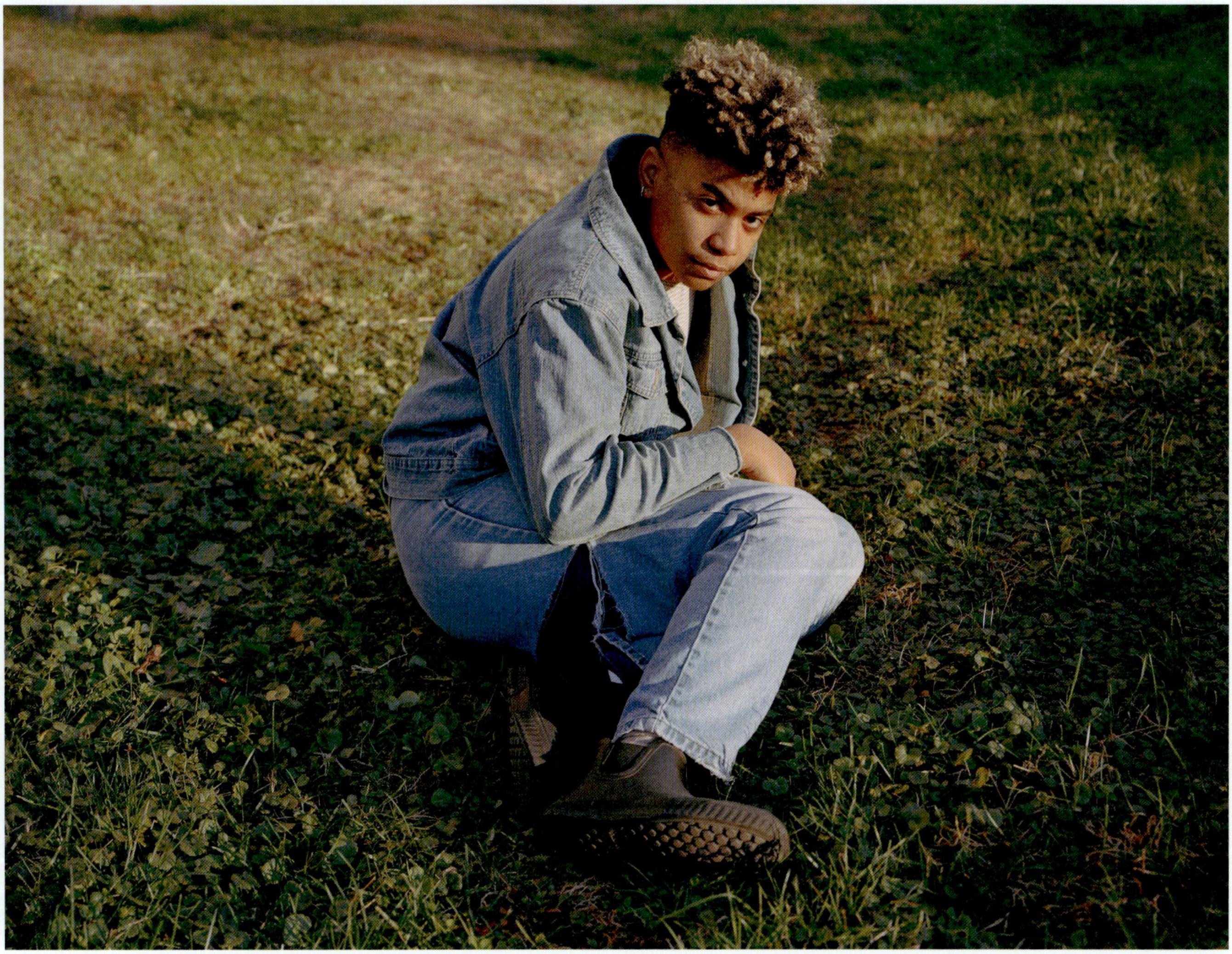

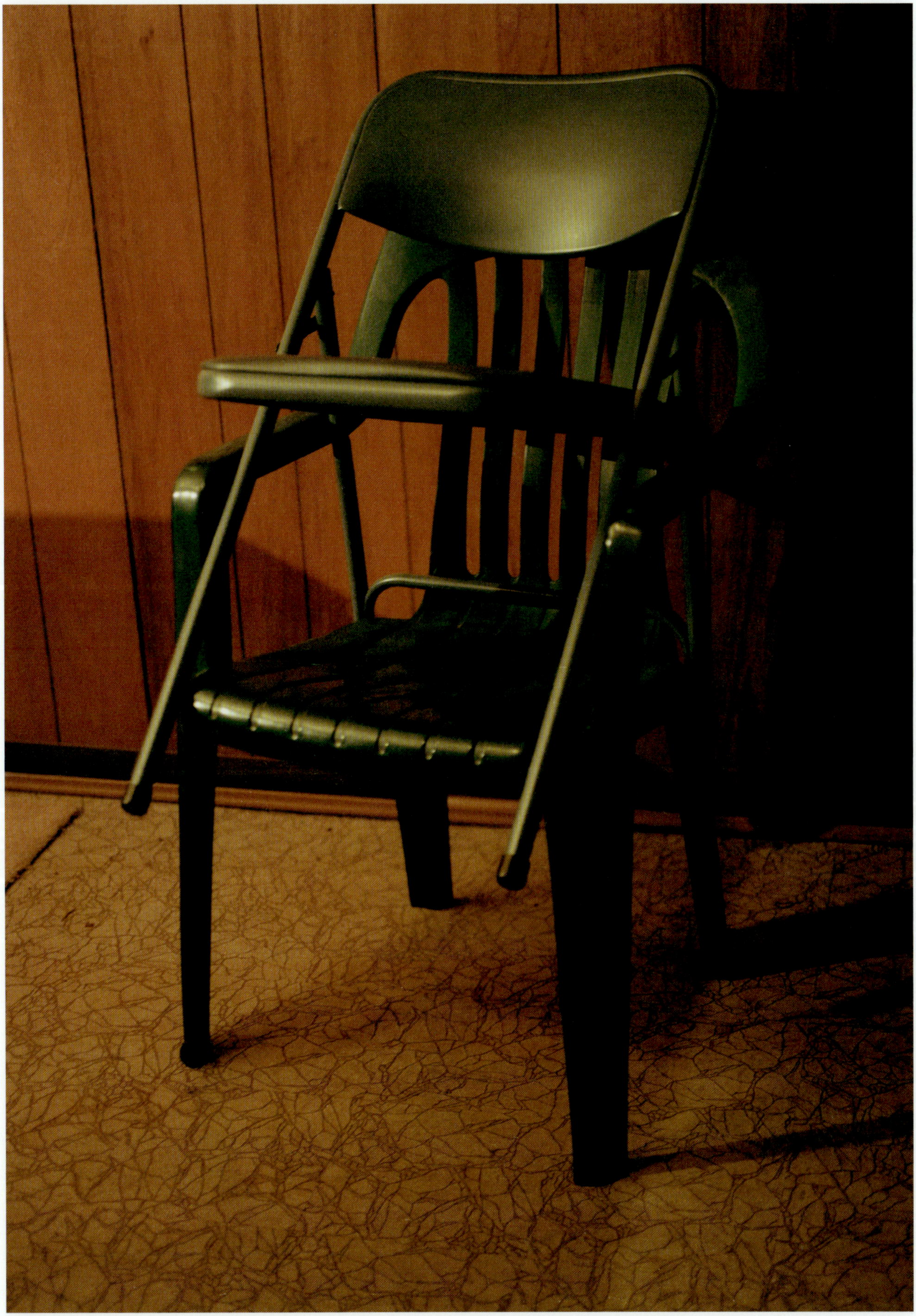

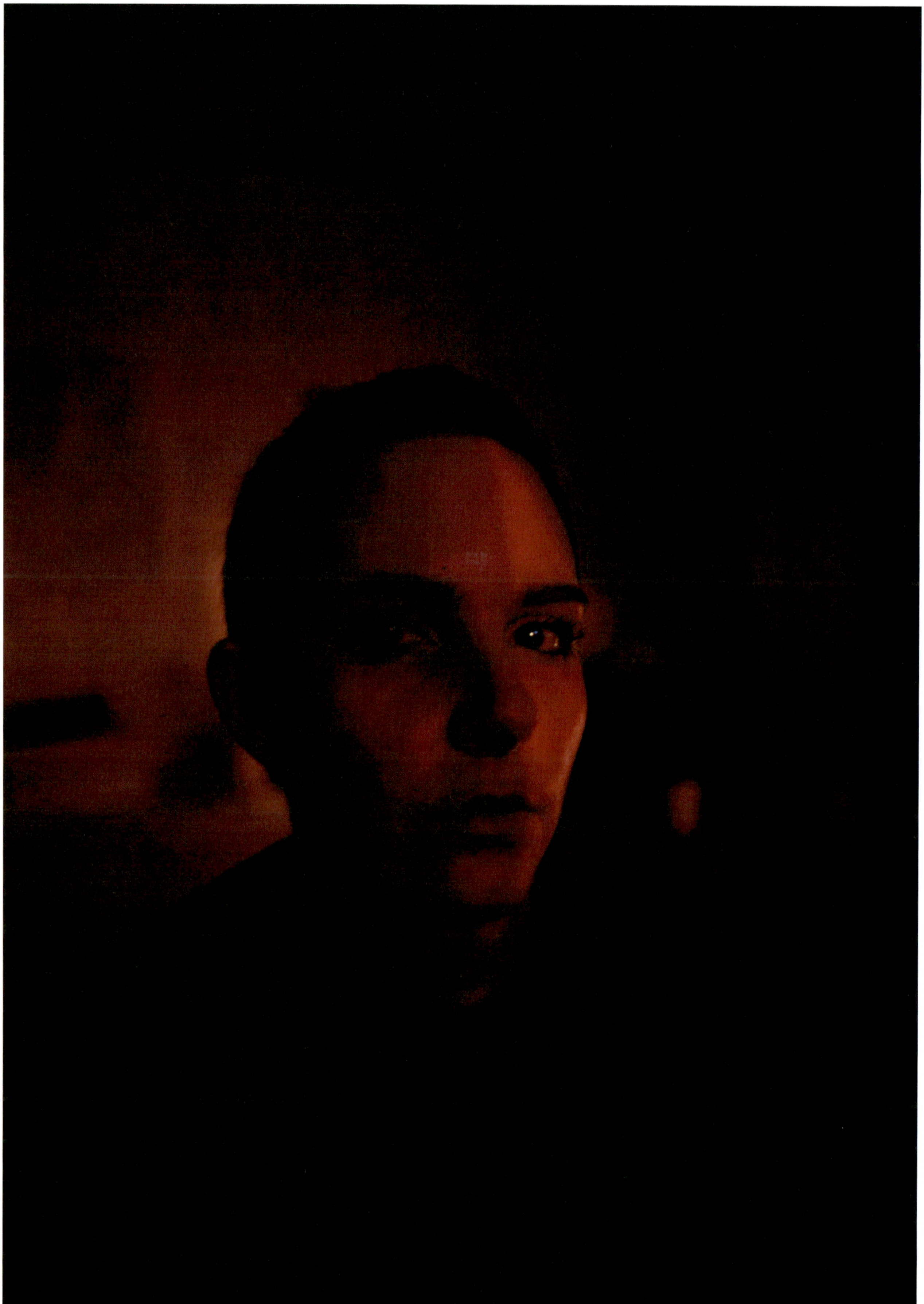

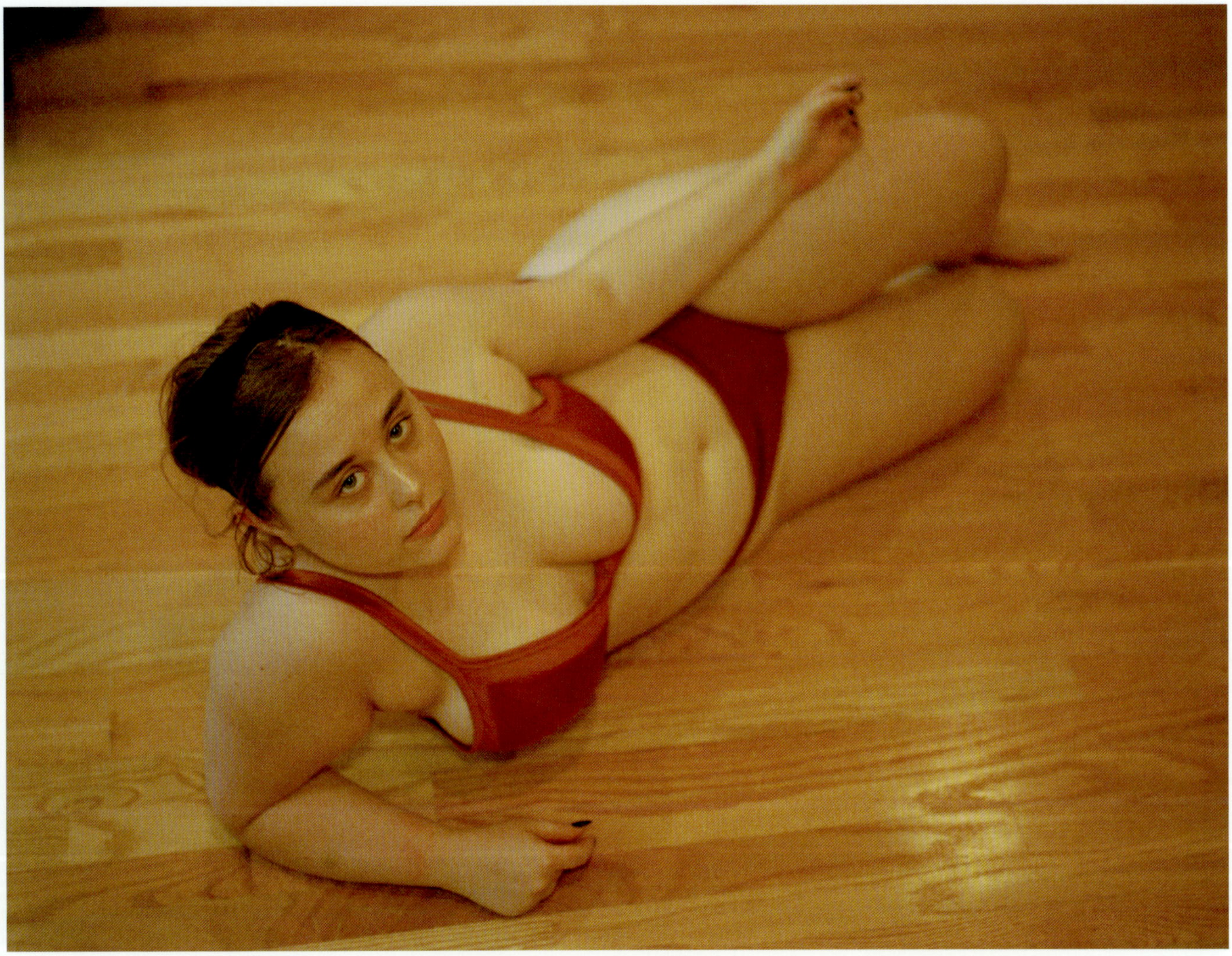

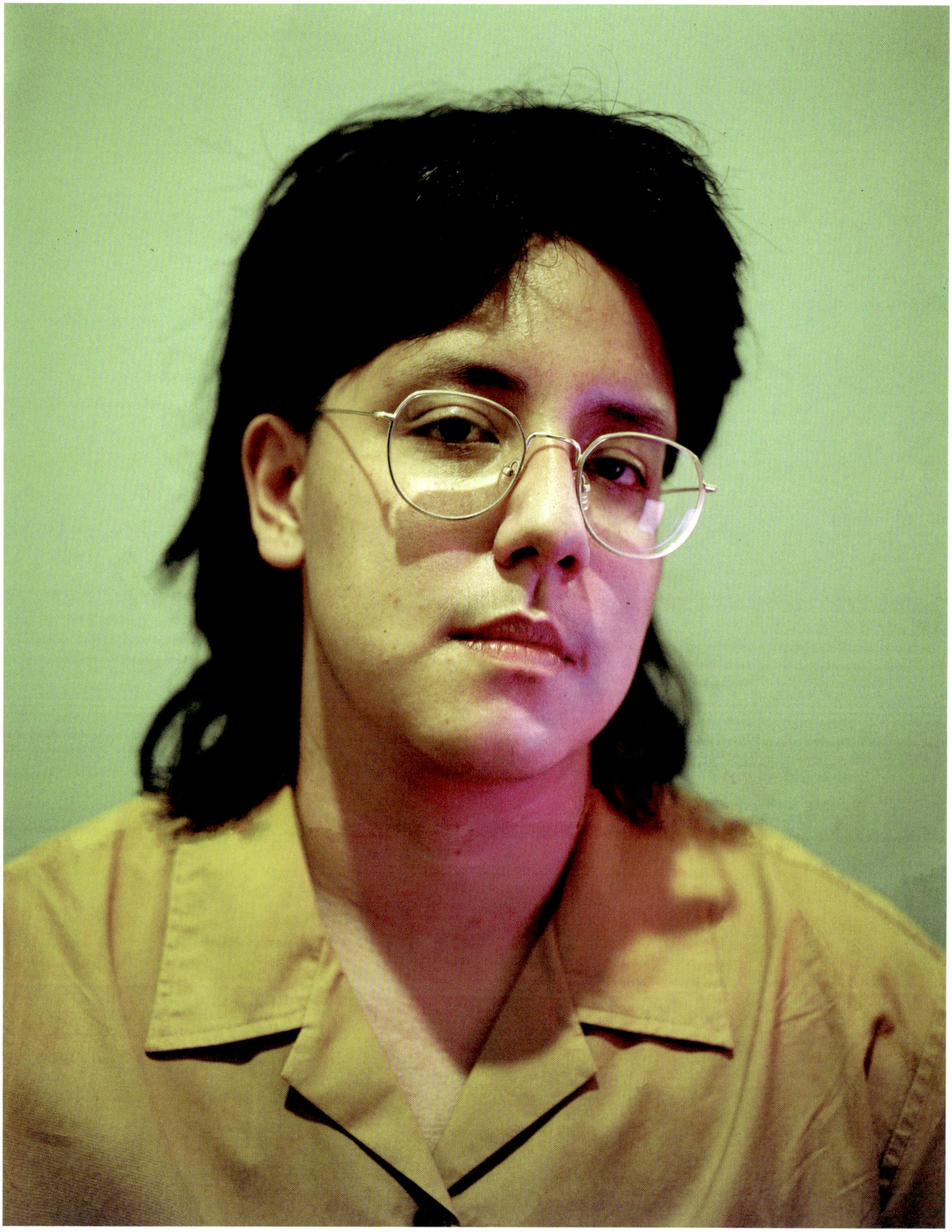

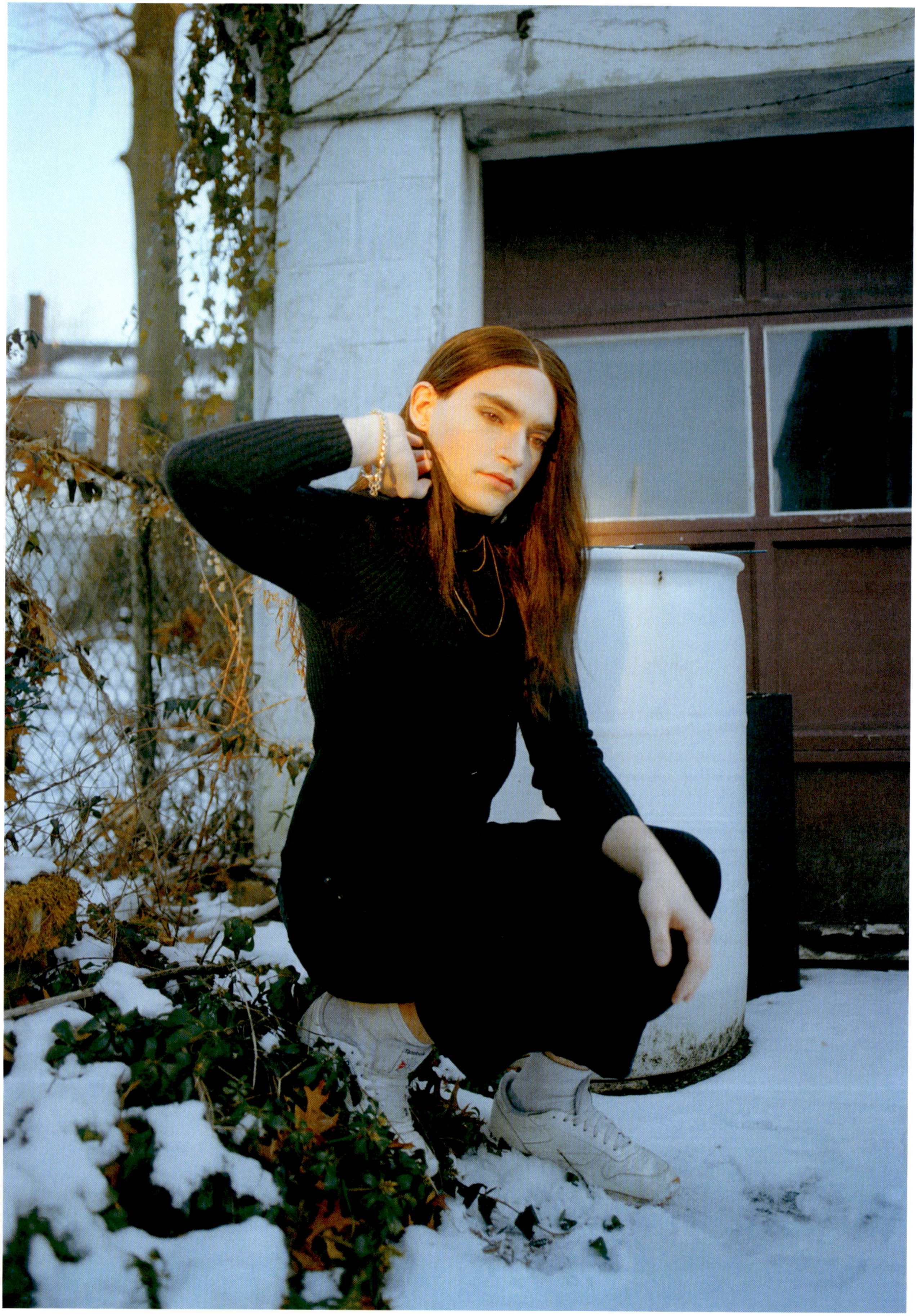

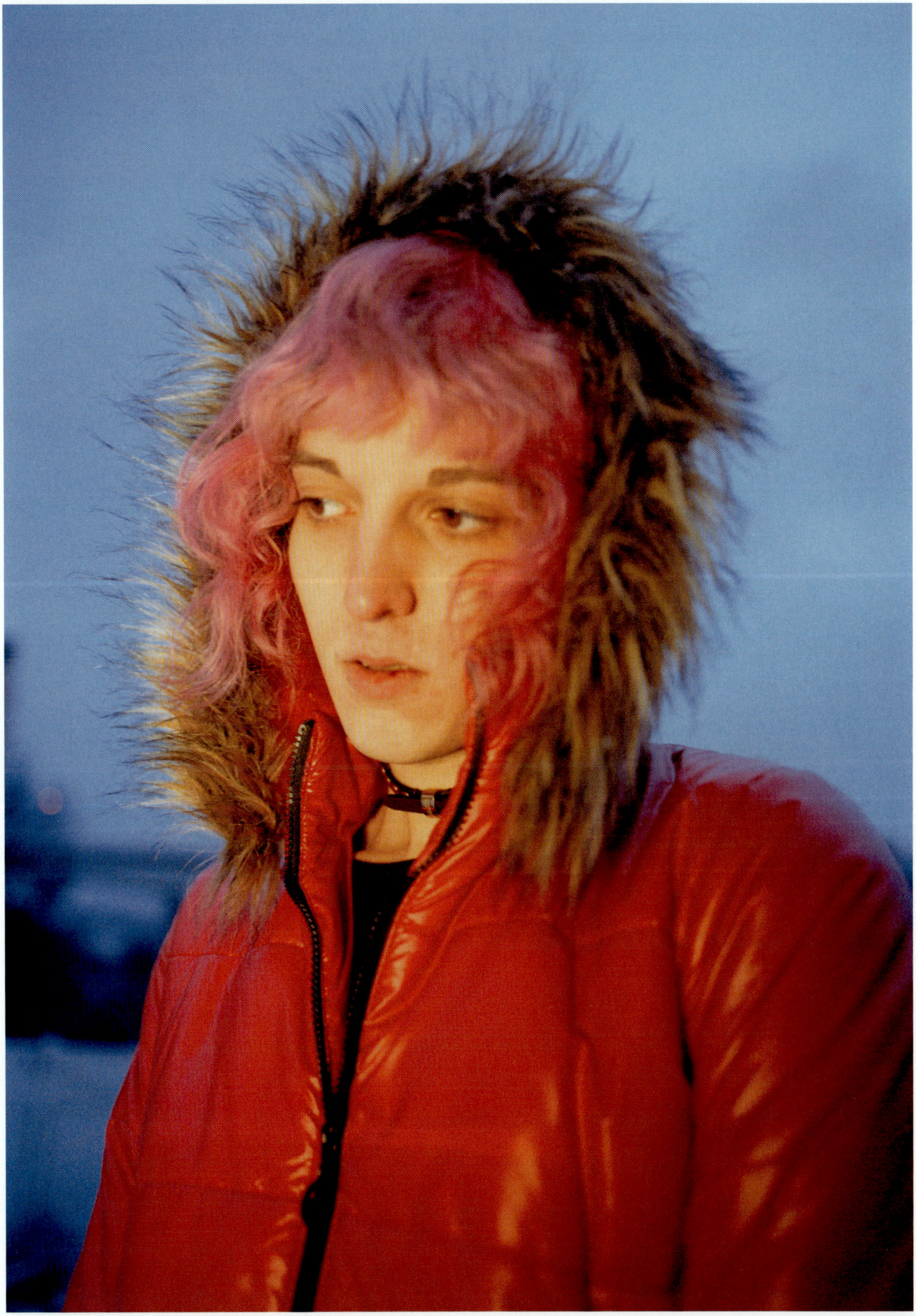

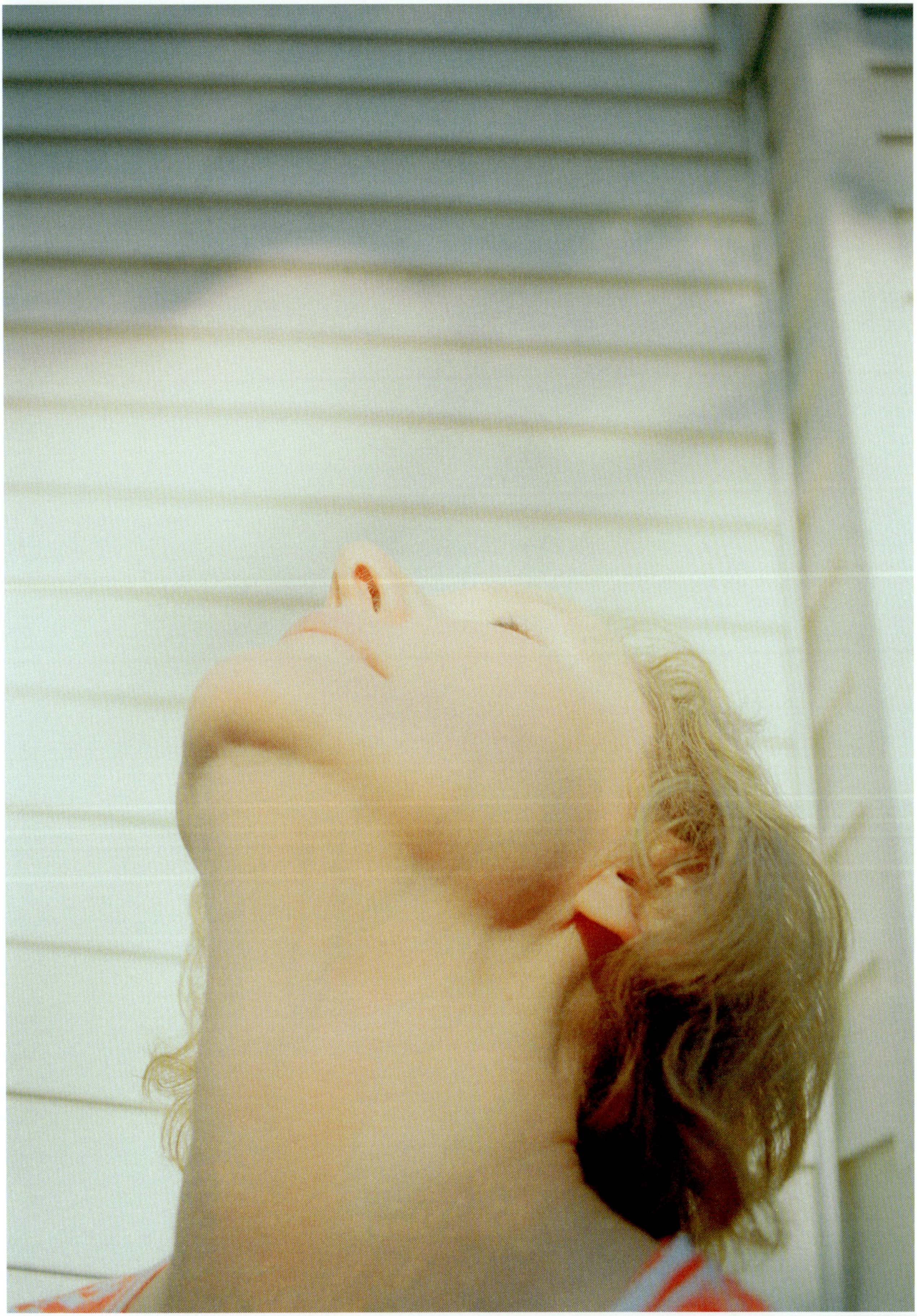

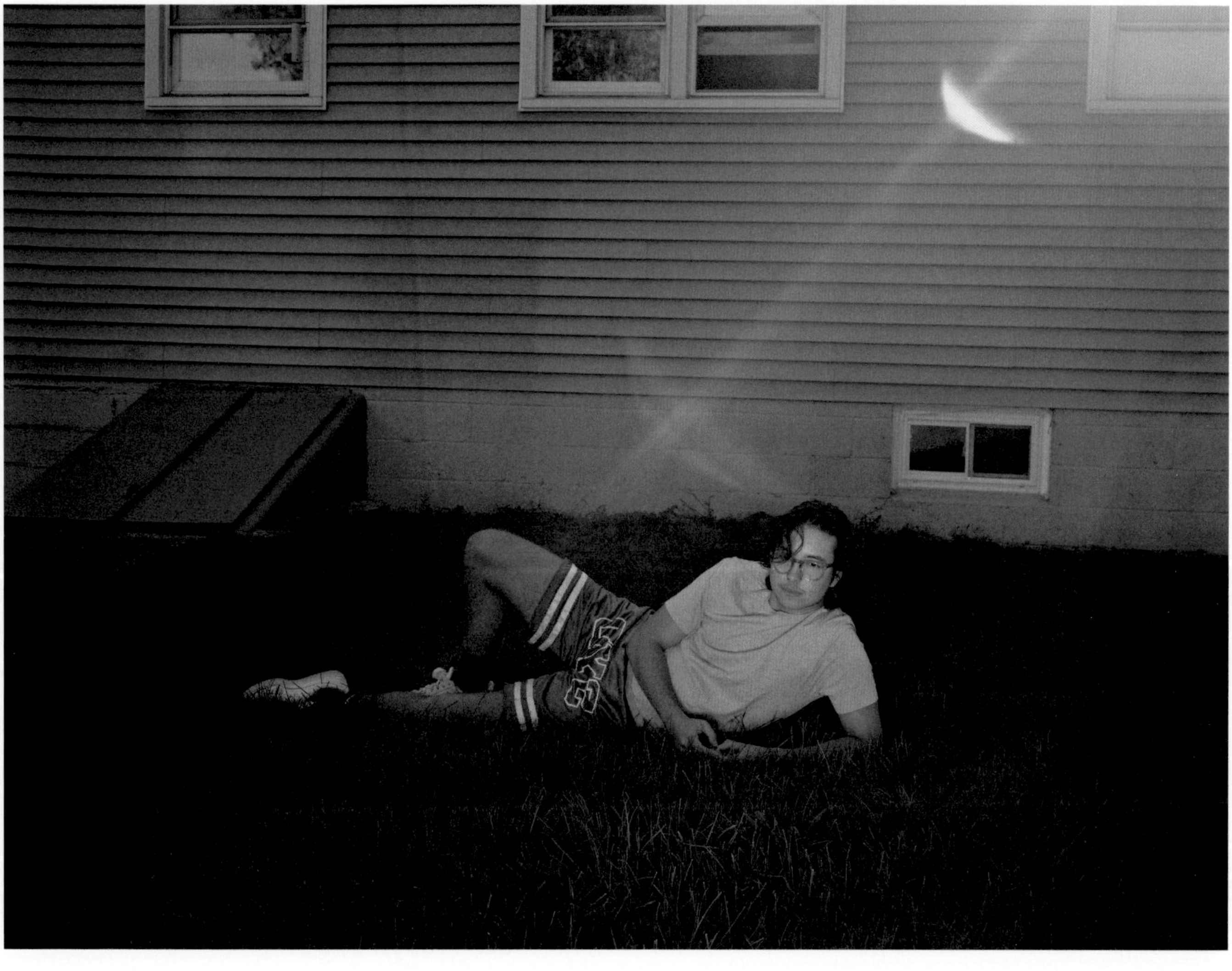

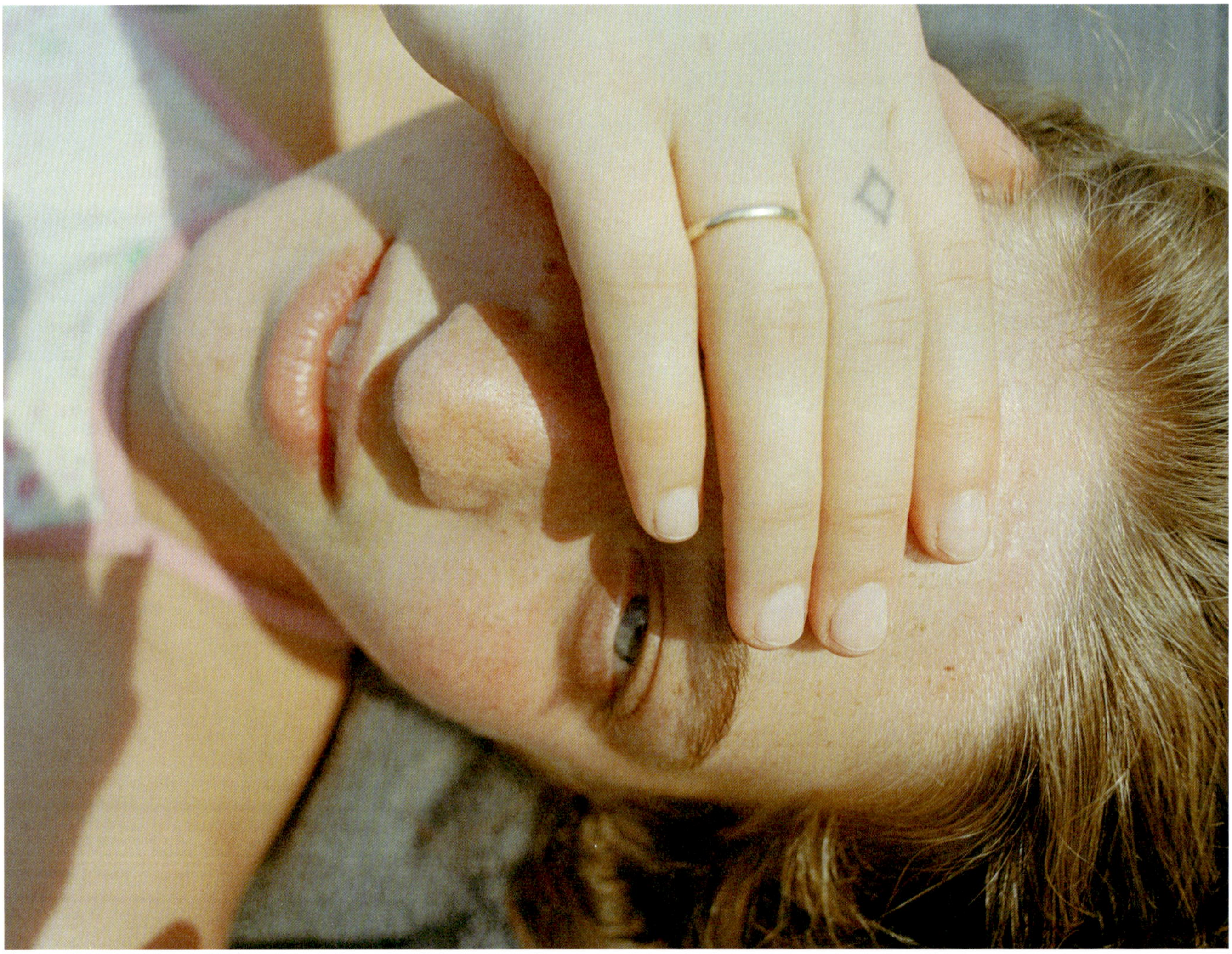

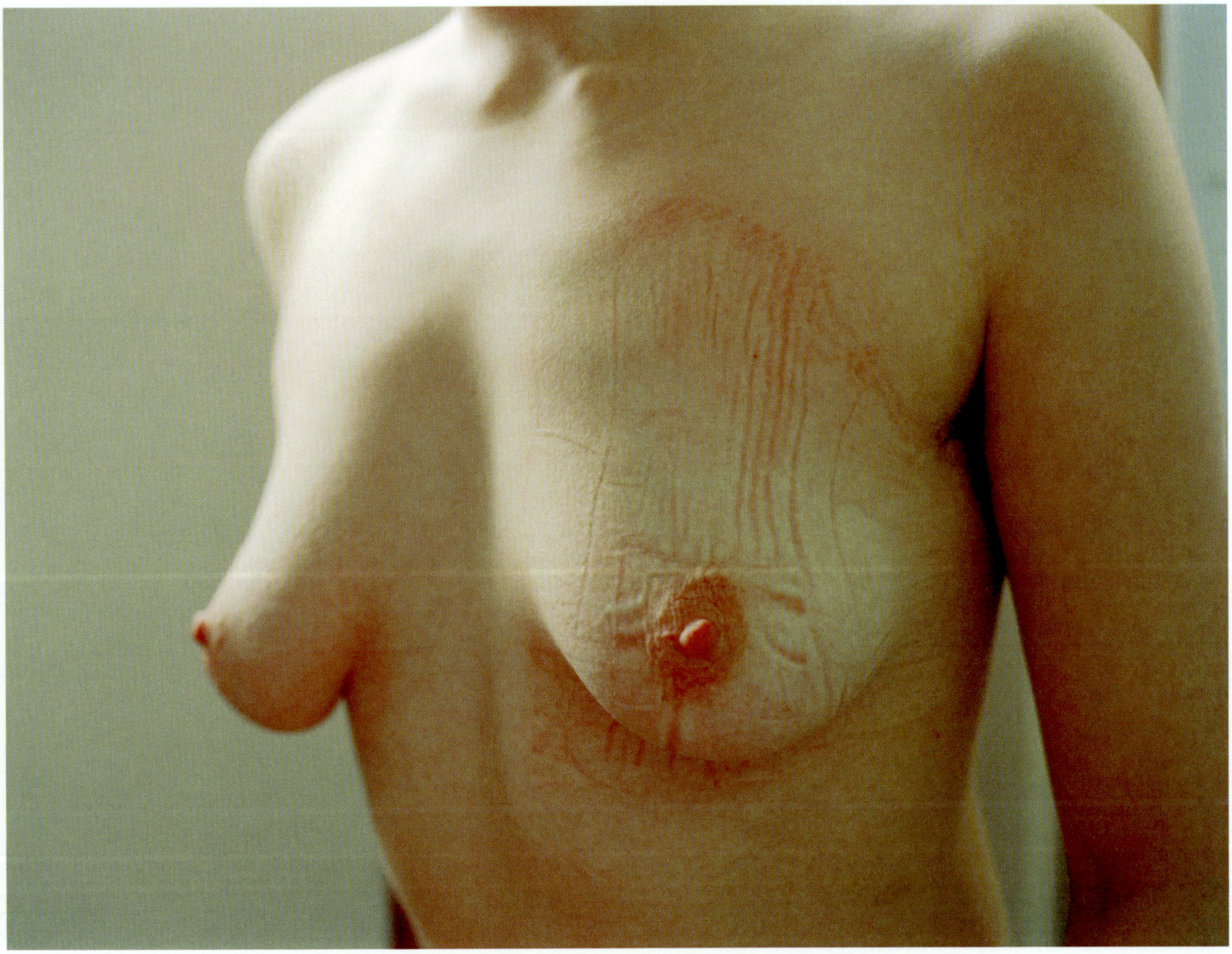

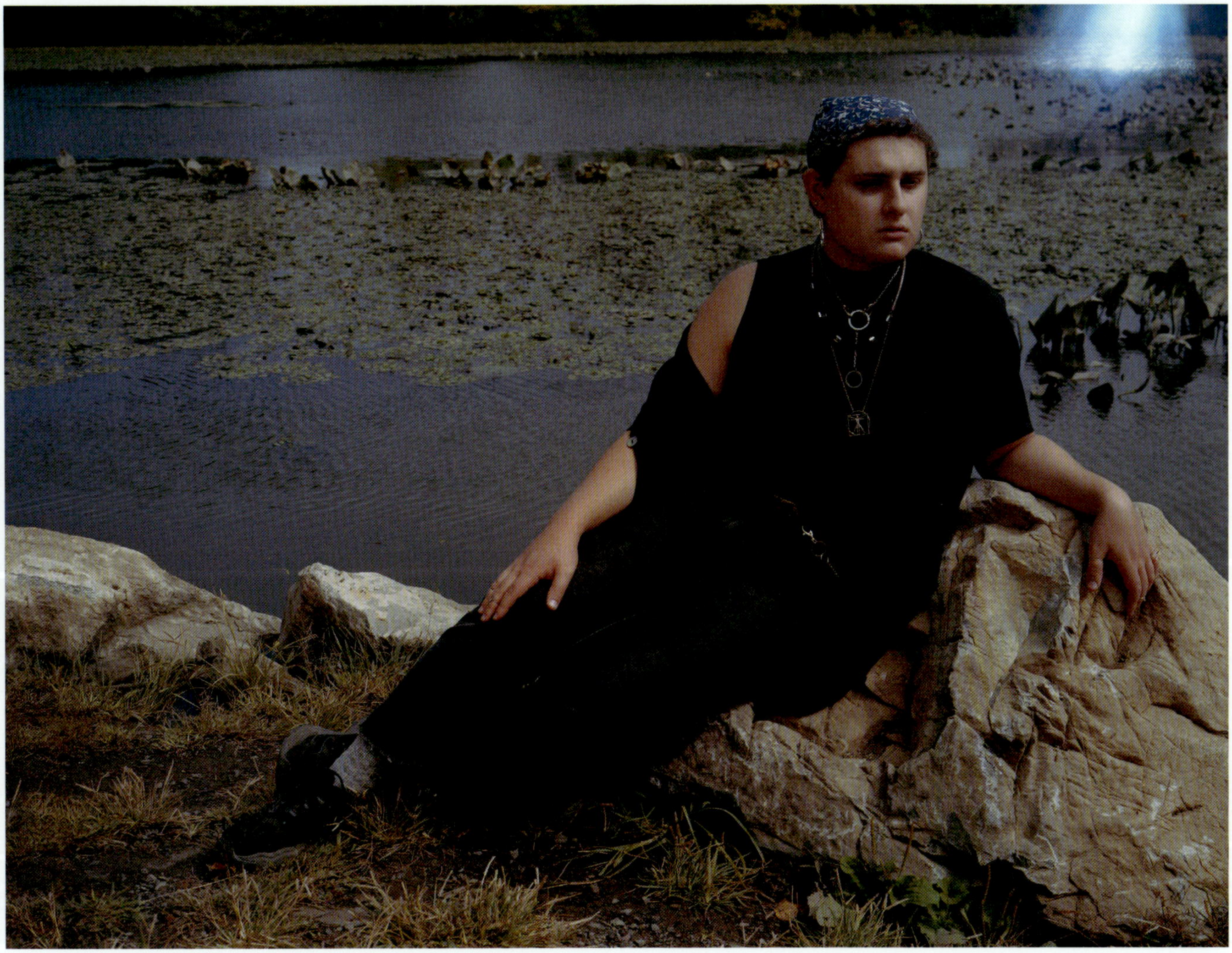

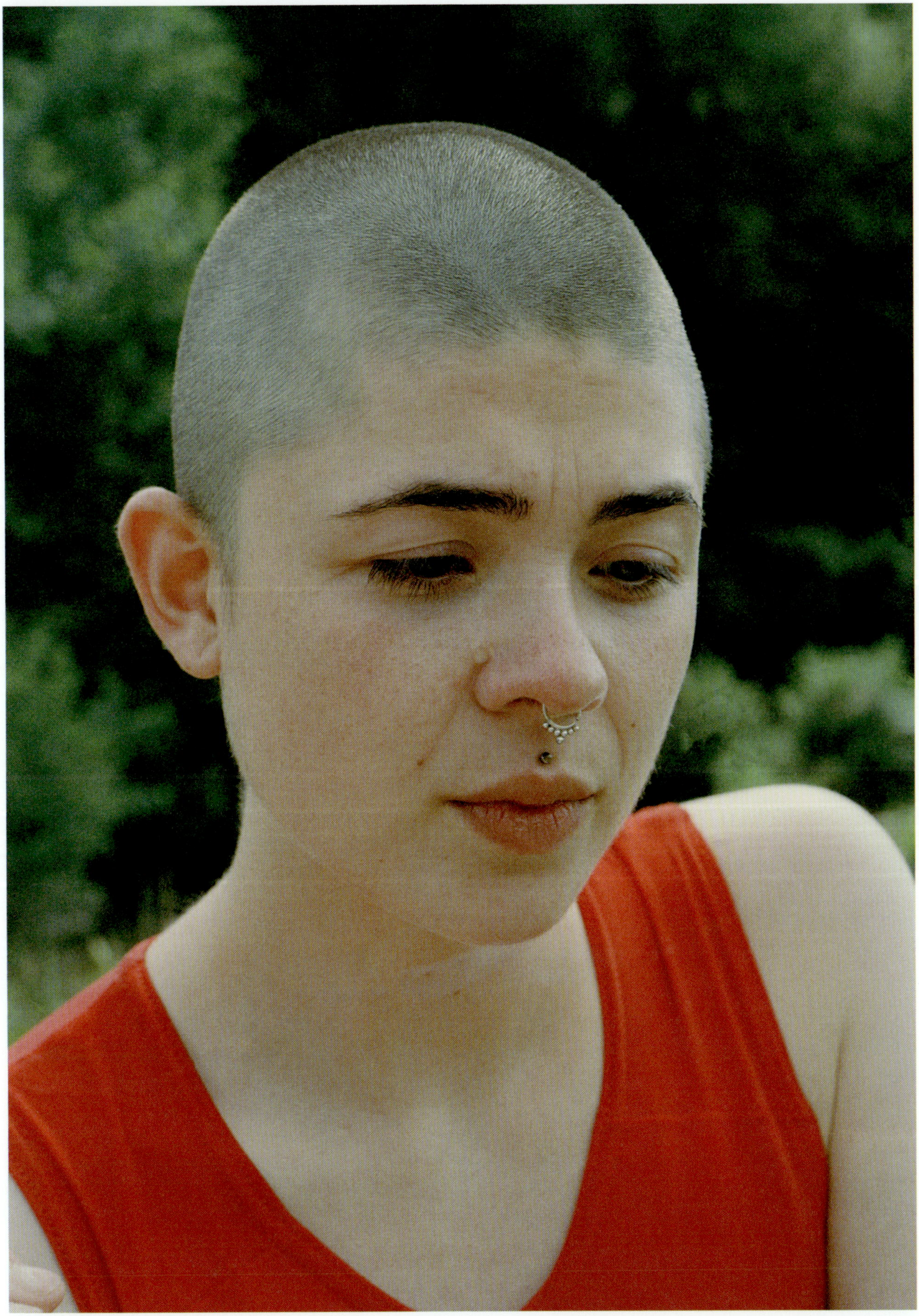

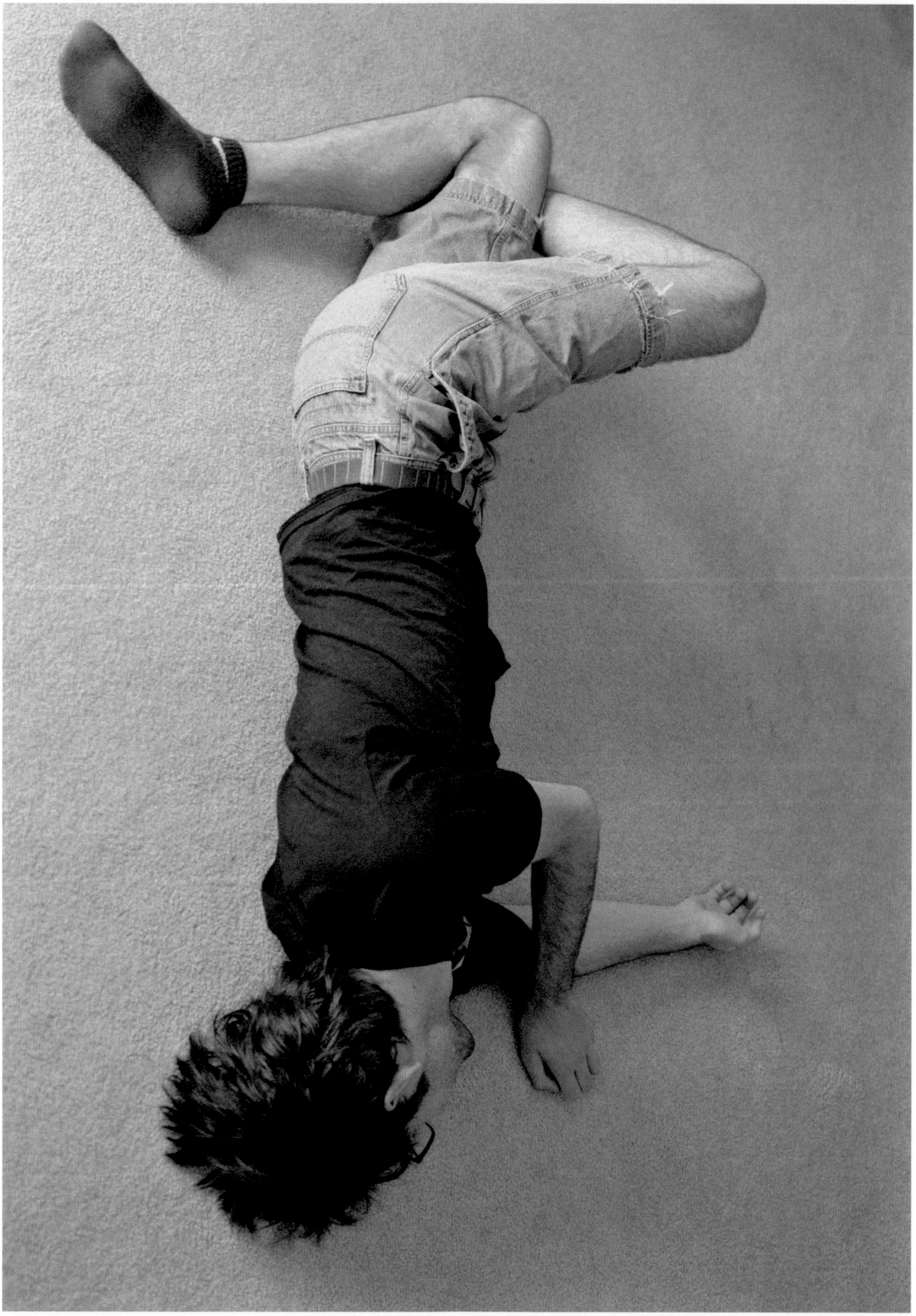

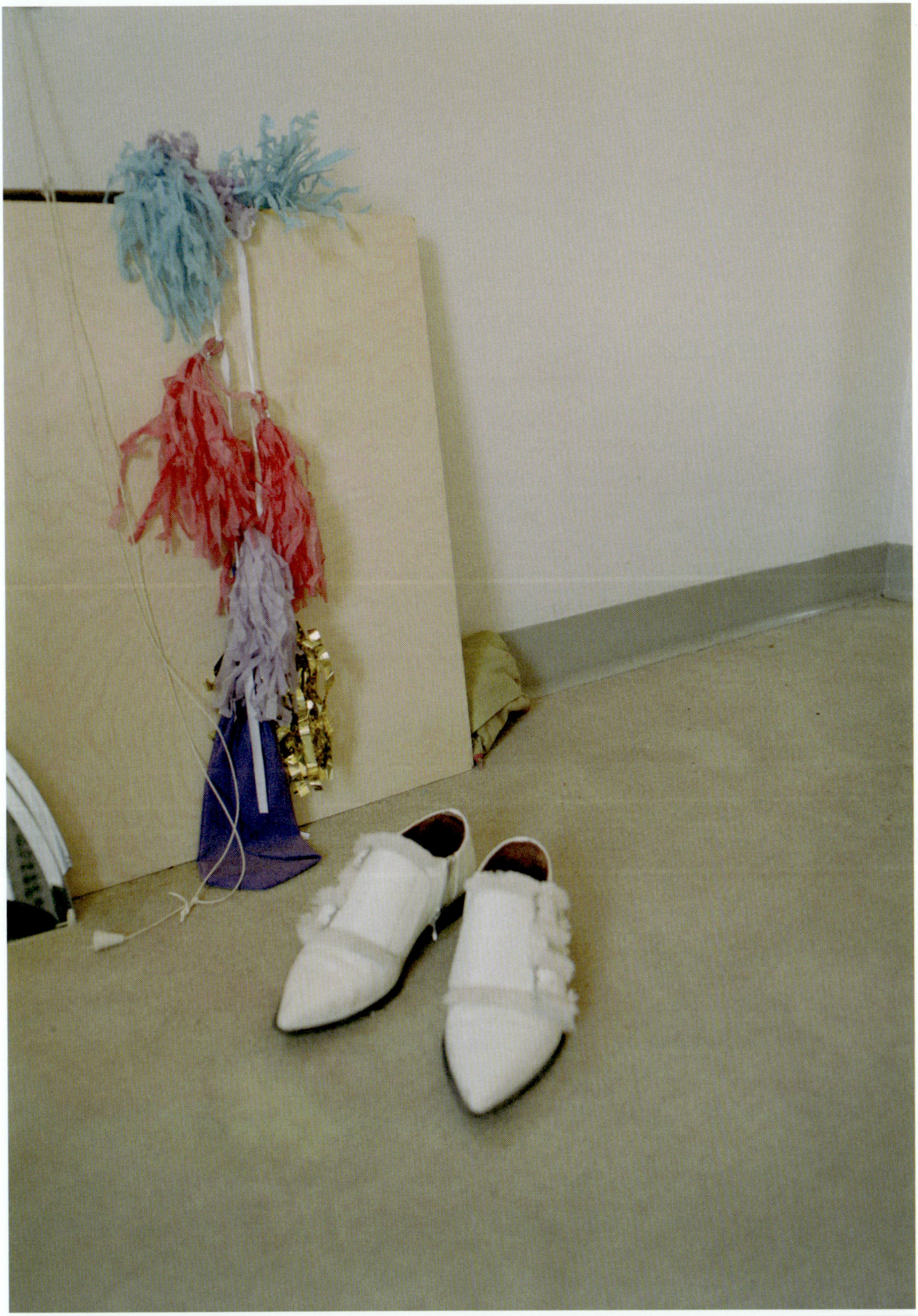

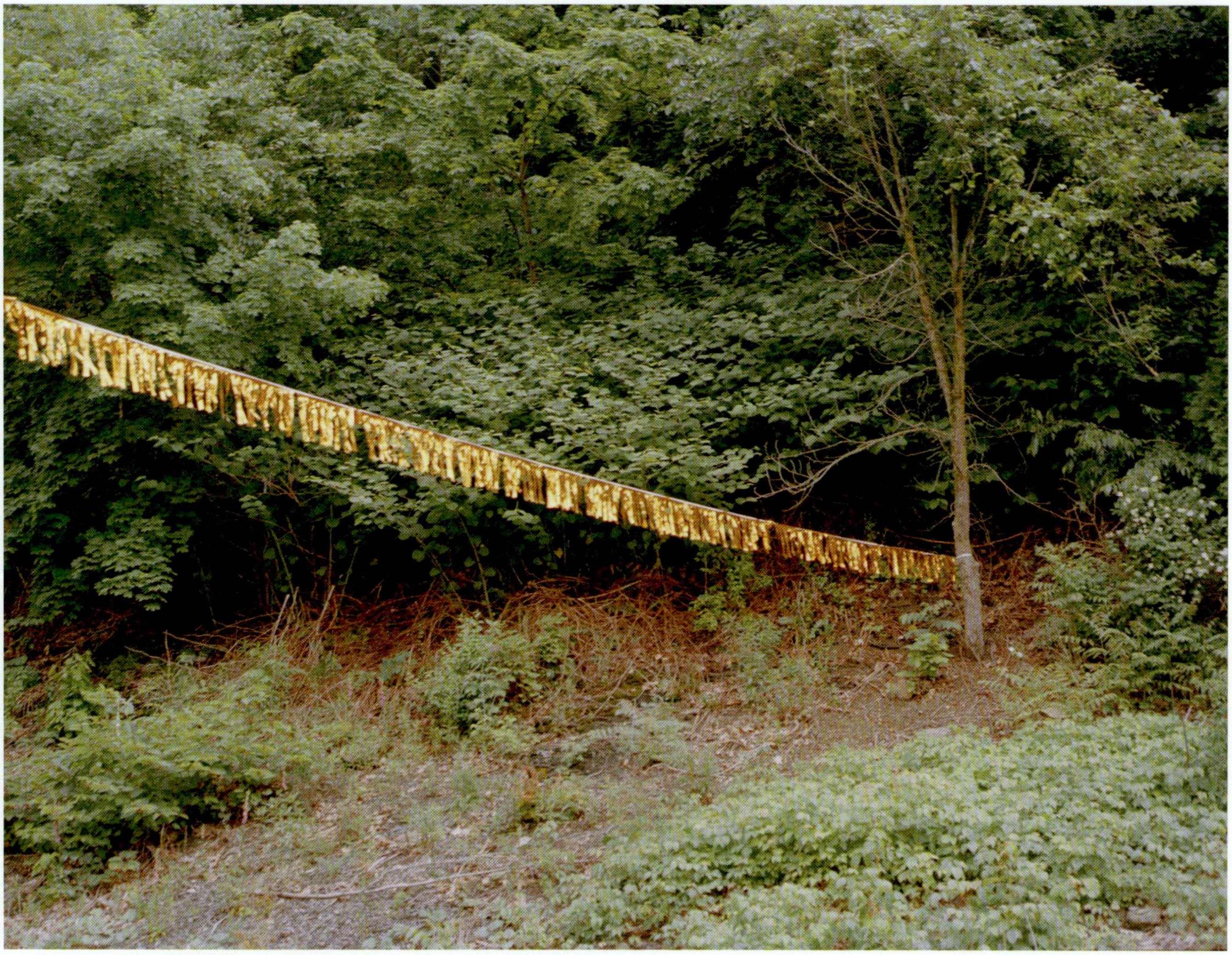

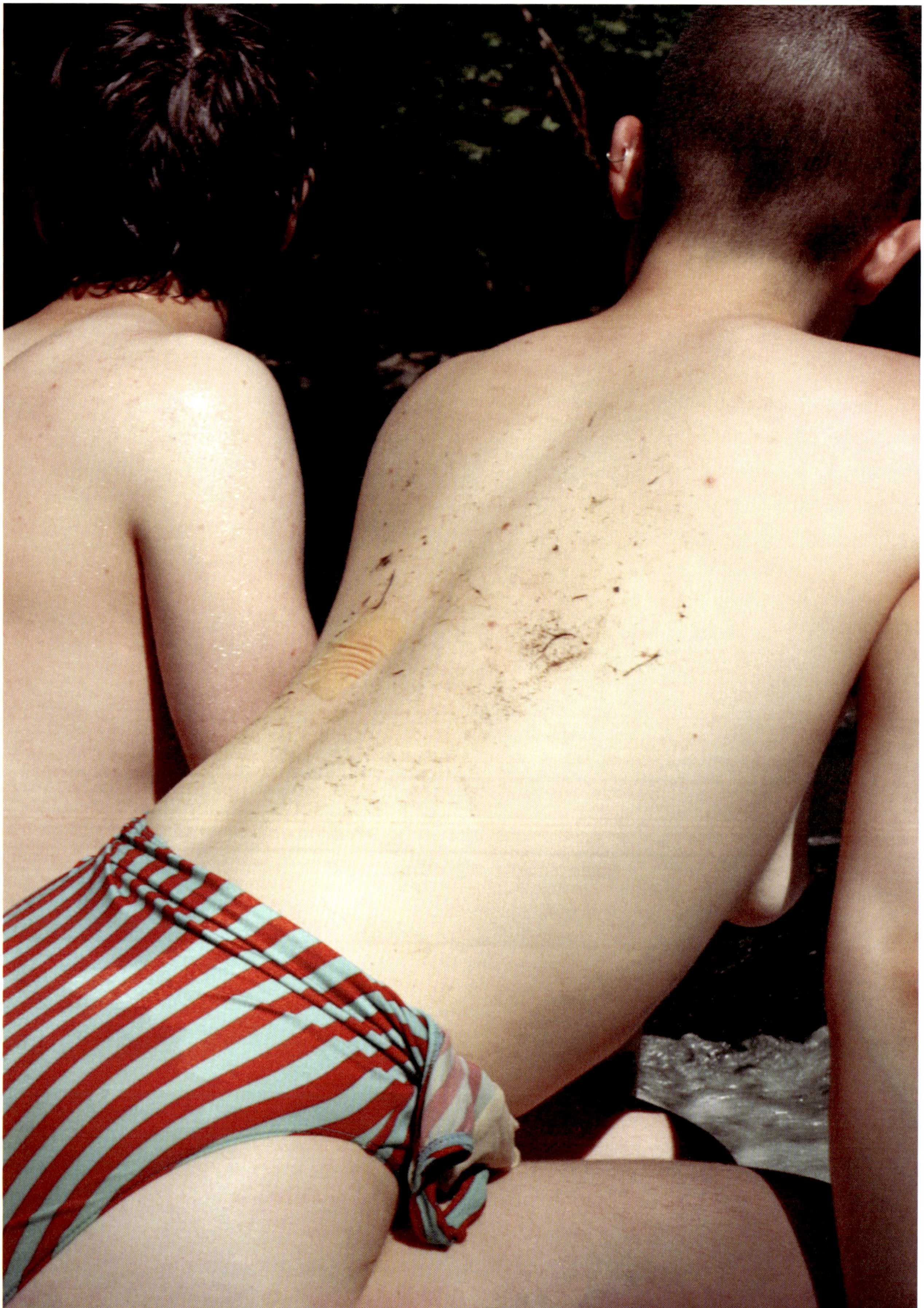

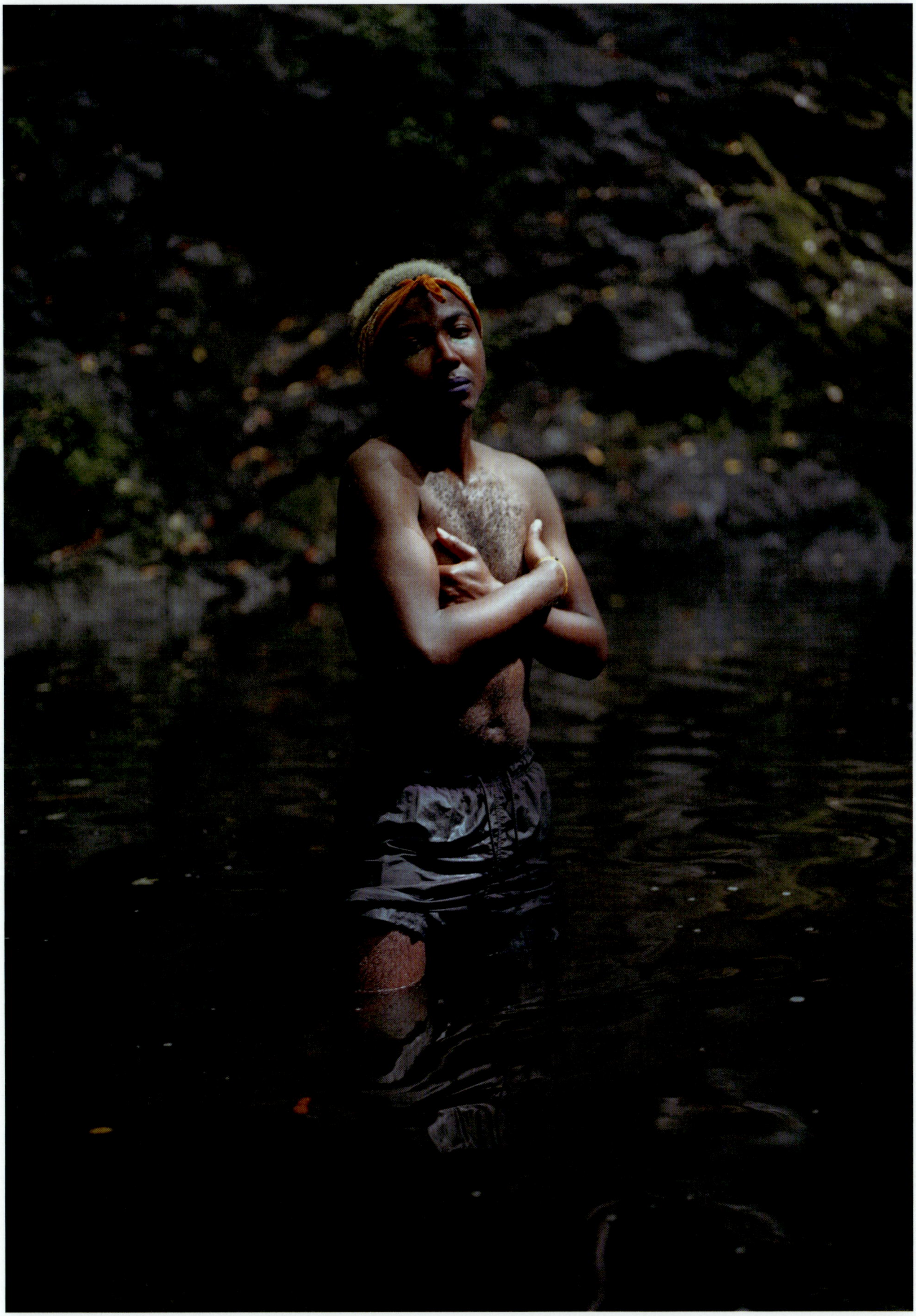

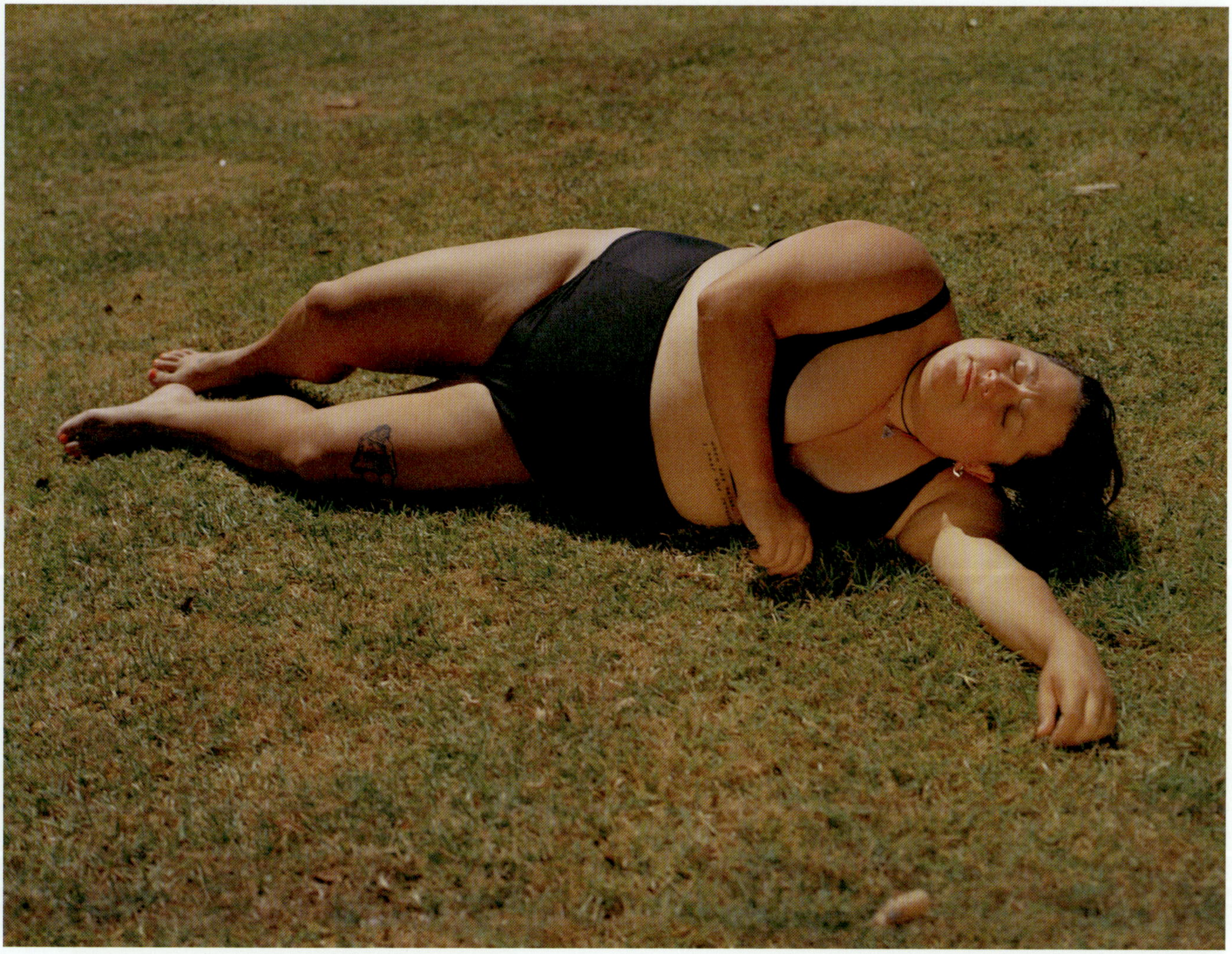

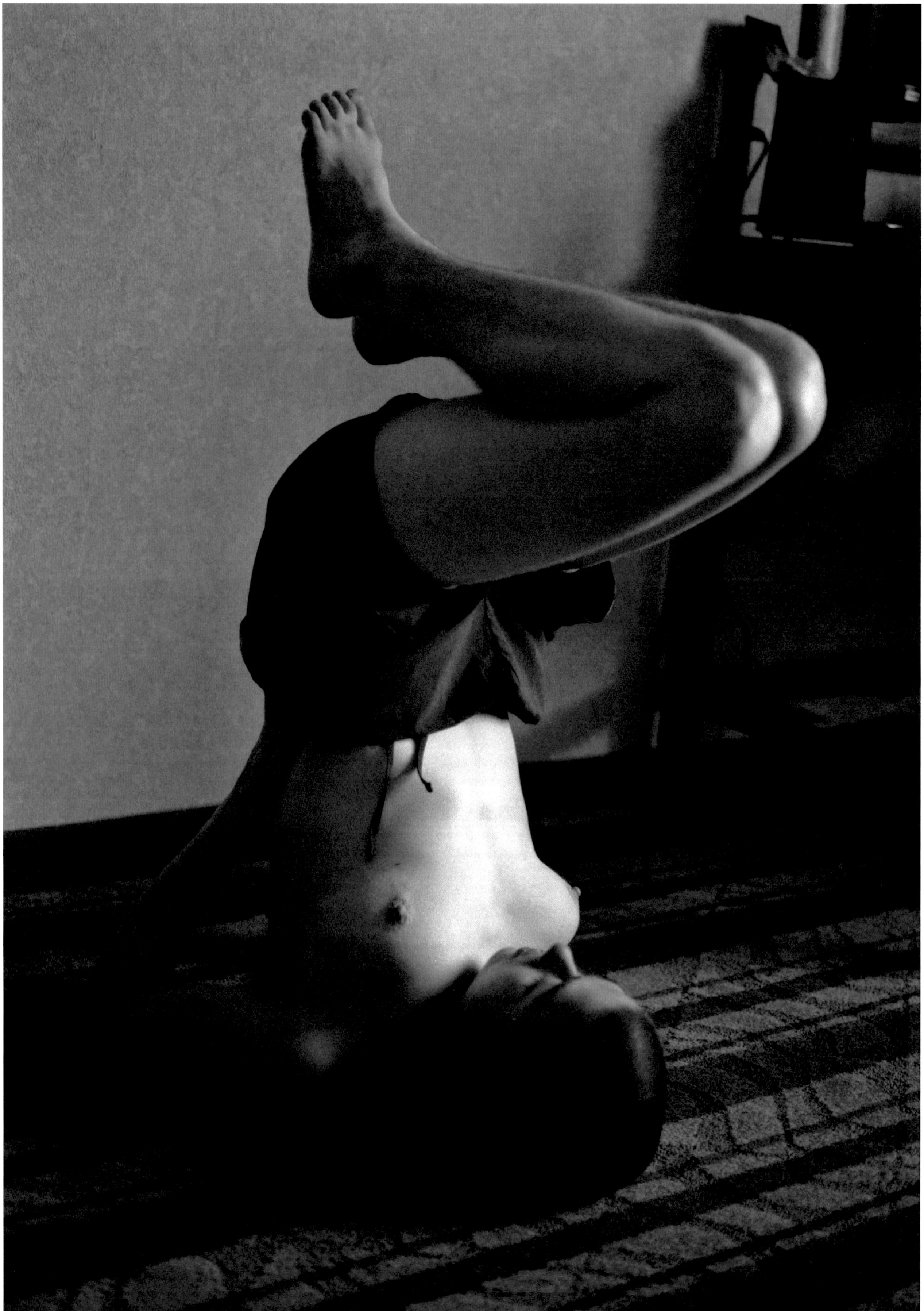

*TUCK AND ROLL (V.);

THE TECHNIQUE, ALMOST ALWAYS DONE WHILE RUNNING, INVOLVES DIVING FORWARD IN SUCH A WAY THAT YOUR SHOULDER LANDS ON THE GROUND FIRST, AND YOU ROLL INTO A SMALL BALL. AS YOU COME OUT OF THE BALL, IMMEDIATELY SPRING BACK UP INTO A RUNNING STANCE, OR, MOVE INTO A KNEELING POSITION.

IMAGE INDEX (TUCK + ROLL)

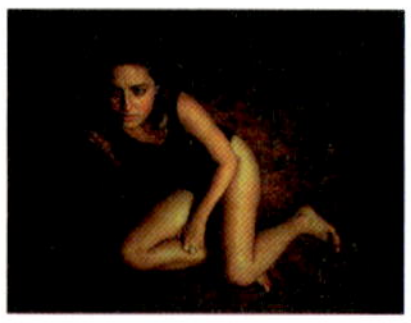

X 01 ELLA DURING THE STORM (2018)

2019.01 ?

WHERE IS THIS NEGATIVE

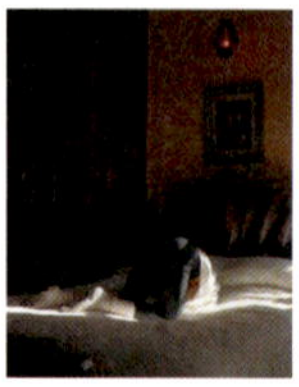

X 02 ALEEM AT THE PARADOR (2021)

2021.06

hotel_45001.jpg

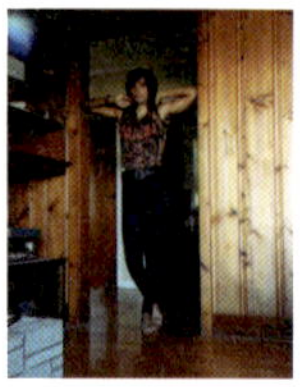

X 03 ARI (2020)

2020.09

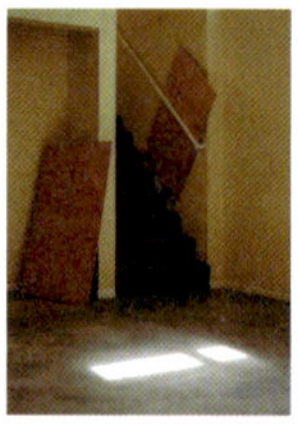

X 04 THE APARTMENT I MET NYALLAH IN (2017 ?)

OLD

NEED FILE

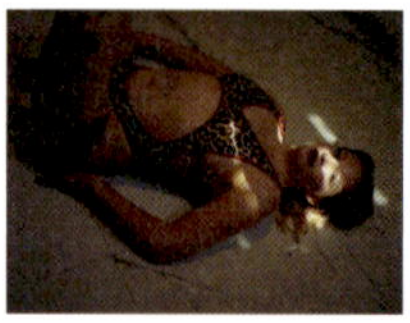

X ~~05~~ LEX ON THEIR KITCHEN FLOOR ~~(2020)~~ (2021)

2021.06

lex26.jpg

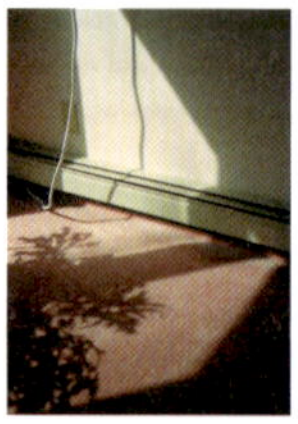

X 06 ALEEM'S GRANDMOTHER'S BEDROOM'S CARPET (20[illegible]) 19

MICHIGAN SCANS

605.03.carpet_revised.jpg

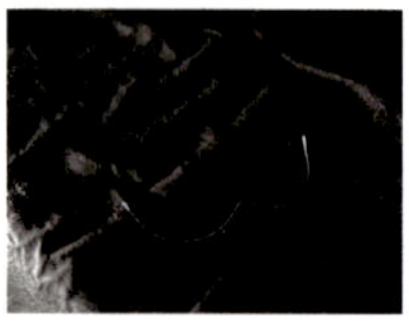

X ~~07~~ UNDERWIRE (PRE-OP) SELF-PORTRAIT ON OCEAN AVE ~~(2019)~~ (2020)

~~2021~~

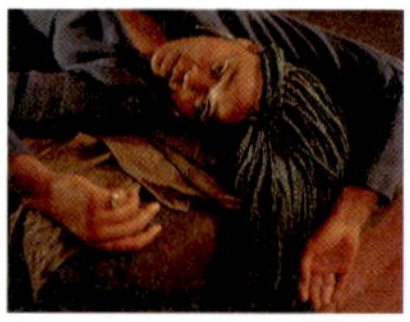

08

2021.03 NYALLAH IN MY APARTMENT ~~(2022)~~ (2021)

nyl2.jpg

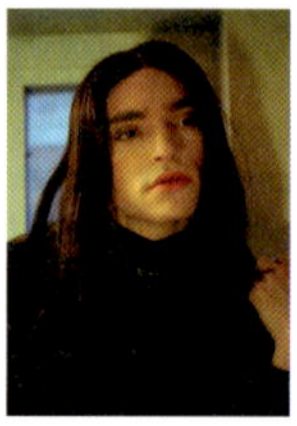

X ~~09~~ GEEP IN THEIR BATHROOM (2018)

2020.05

edit16

WHERE IS THIS NEGATIVE

INDEX 02

X 10 MAXWELL (2020)
2020.09

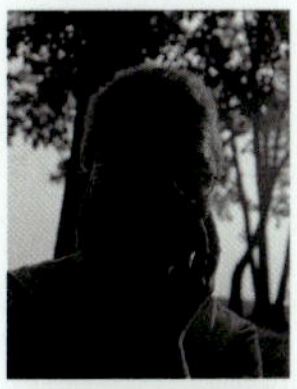

X 11 ALEEM IN OUR CAMPER WITH A FRESH SHAVE (2020)

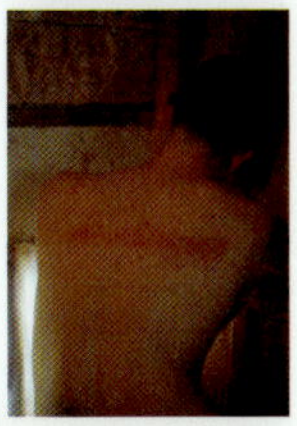

X 12 TONI CUTTING ELLAS HAIR (2018)

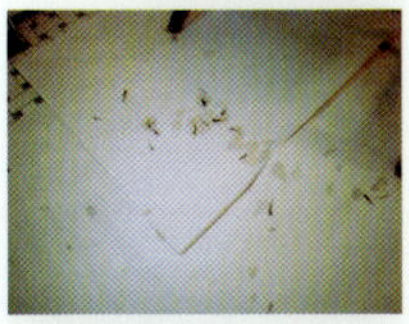

2019
X 13 ASHER POST-OP (POSED BY TAY) "THE EUPHORIA I SOUGHT OUT WITH THIS SURGERY" (2020)
2020.09

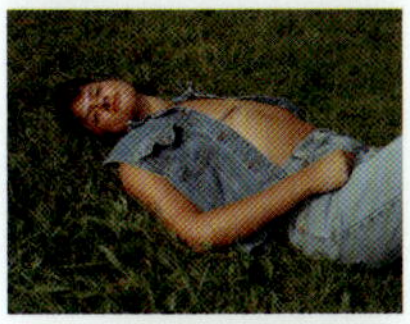

"ARTIST + DISABILITY ACTIVIST SUNAURA TAYLOR SAID 'WHEN BETWEEN MALE + FEMALE OR BETWEEN DEATH + HEALTH, DO YOU STILL COUNT AS HUMAN?' THE INTERSECTIONS OF THOSE EXPERIENCES HAVE BEEN HEAVY ON MY MIND DURING MY HEALING."

X 14 ~~SHANNON~~ ON THE ROOF PRINCESS ~~(2018)~~ (2019)
2019.08
shannon09.jpg

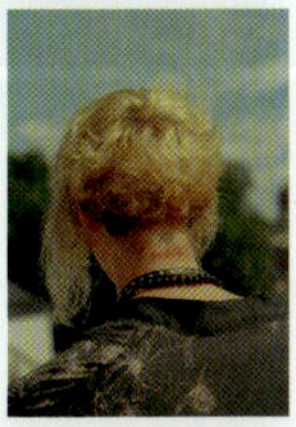

X 15 RACHEL BASKING (2018)
2019.08

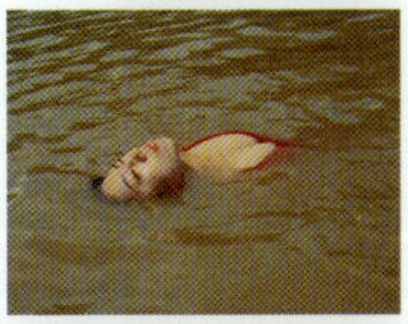

16 CHRISTINE AT THE POOL (2018)

MY FILM GOT LOST IN THE MAIL AND I REMEMBER CHRISTINE AGAIN PICKING THE BUGS OUT THE POOL SO WE COULD REMAKE THIS PICTURE BEFORE SHE MOVED

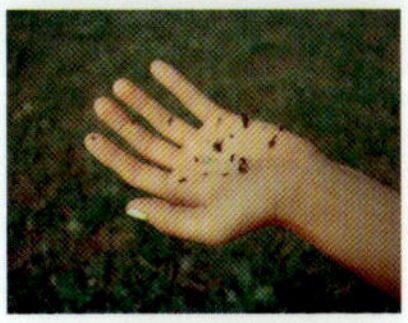

X 17 MYHA'LA AT DUSK ON THE ROOF (BABYGIRL) (2016)
2018.09

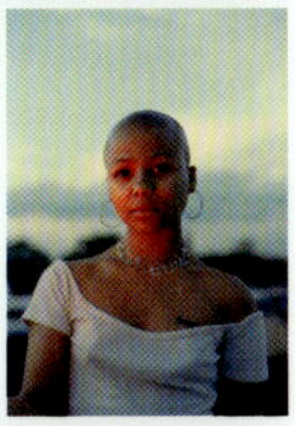

NEED FILE
X 18 JUSTICE IN YELLOW (2020)
(OUTSIDE [redacted] LIBRARY/PARKING LOT)

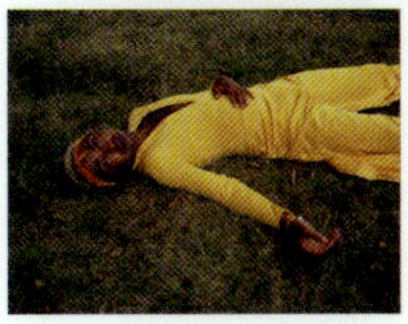

INDEX 03

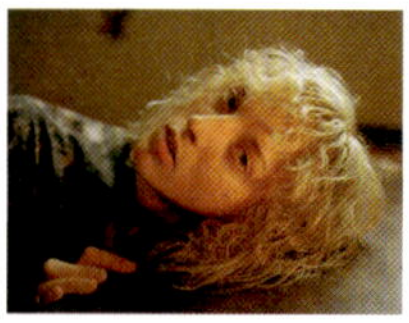

X 19 SHANNON ON THE KITCHEN TABLE ~~(2018)~~ (2019)

2019.08 ell.jpg

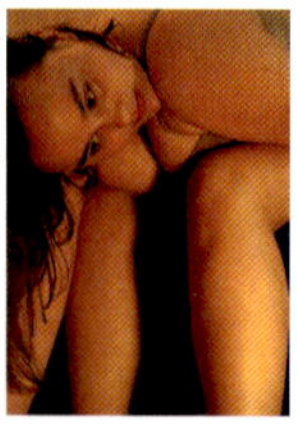

X 20 JENNA (2019)

2019.11 jenna11.jpg

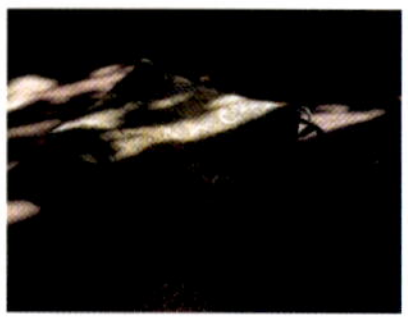

X 21 ALEEM'S GREAT GRANDMOTHER'S CUSHION (2019)

2010.09 MICHIGAN SCANS

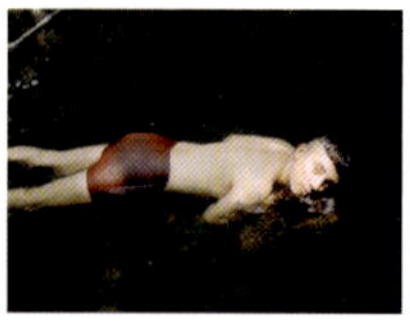

X 22 ÁLE IN THE HUDSON ~~(2018)~~ 2019

2019.06 ale06.jpg

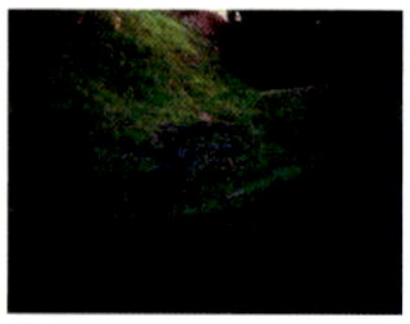

X 23 UNTITLED? (2018)

2020.09 VALLEY IN MONROEVILLE?

BED?

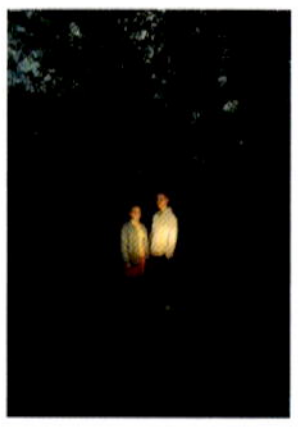

X 24 POSED W JEFF IN MY HEADLIGHTS (2019)

OLD NEED FILE JEFF07.jpg HAVE FINAL TIFF 2019-05

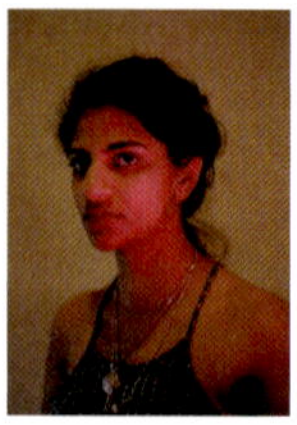

X ✓ 25 RHEA (IN PARENTS) ~~FALL 2020~~ (2019)

2019.11 rhea10.jpg

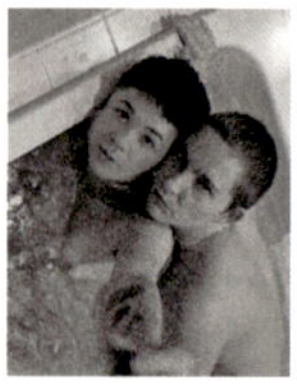

X 26 THE CARLTON INN + LODGE (2020)

2020.11 (SENATOR SUITE) SELF PORTRAIT W ALEEM

WHAT'S THE PRESIDENTIAL SUITE THEN?

april.jpg

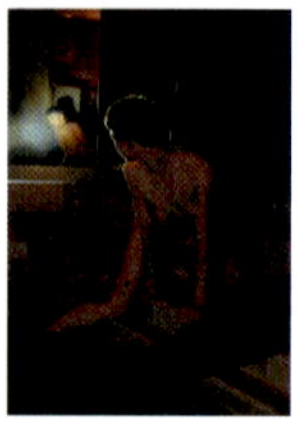

27 PARADISE SPRINGS OR (2022)

COVE HAVEN (CHAMPAGNE SUITE)

DIGITAL - NEW NEED FILE

INDEX 04

OLD NEED FILE

28 PARKER AT THE EDGE OF THE CEMETERY (2020)

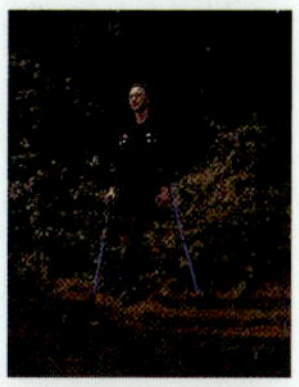

29 TONI (2020)
BEFORE I LEFT

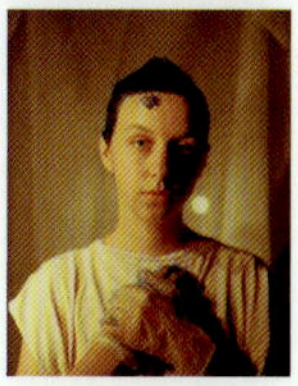

30 FRANCESCO'S FUNERAL (ALEEM'S CHAIR) (20[illegible]) 20
2020.05 edit16

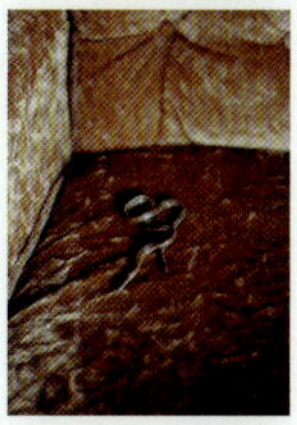

31 JAY (2017?)
2019.11

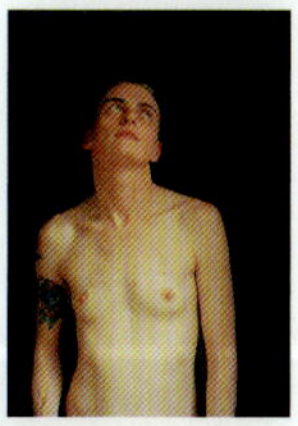

32 EMMA ON MY LONG COUCH (2018)
2019.09

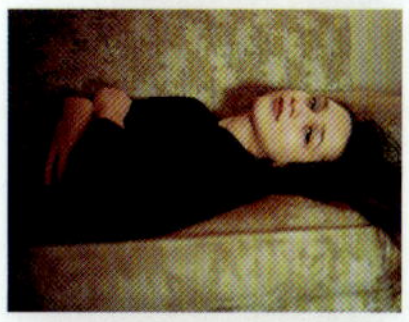

33 MILO IN THE EVENING (2020)
2020.09

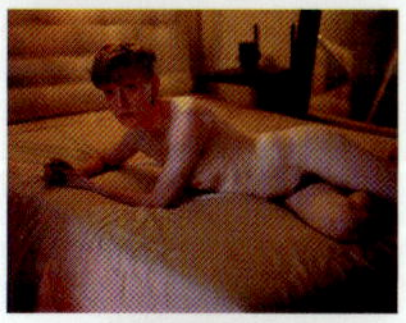

34 MEETING ~~SOPHIA~~ SOPHIE (2017)
2020 ARCHIVE SELECTS

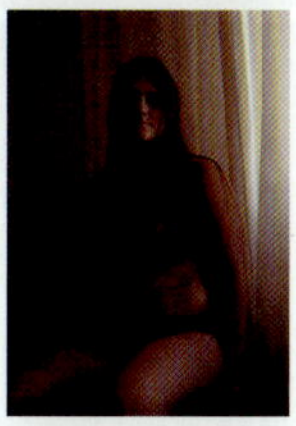

35 LILY (2018)
2019.10

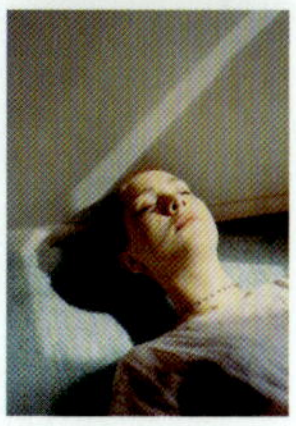

INDEX 05

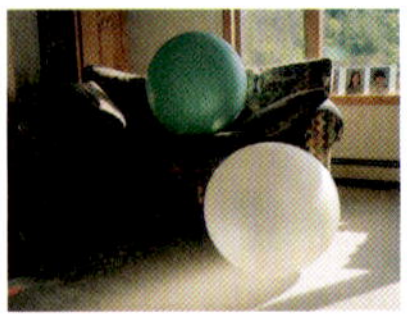

36 ALEEM + BRAN IN THEIR GRANDMOTHER'S COUCH IN THE AFTERNOON (2019)

MICHIGAN SCANS

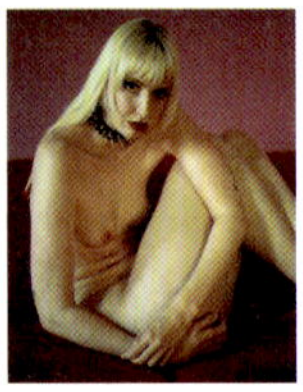

NEW(?) NEED FILE - SW FOLDER?

X 37 JANNA ON THEIR COUCH ~~(2022)~~ ~~(2021)~~ (2020)

2020.09 janna10.jpg

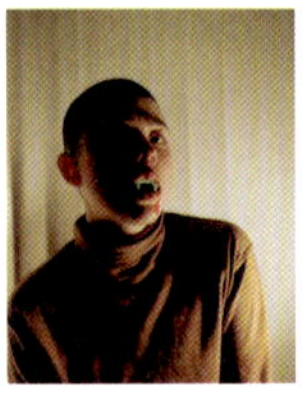

X 38 VAMPIRE ALEEM ~~(2020)~~ 2019

2019.12

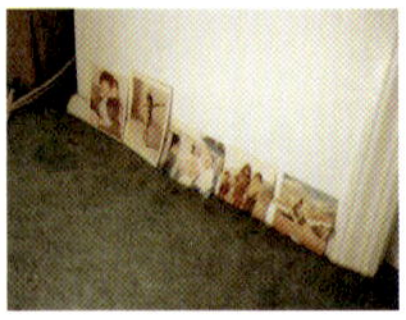

X 39 COLLECTED FAMILY PHOTOS OF OTHER FAMILIES IN LILY'S ROOM (2018)

NEED FILE

edit25.jpg

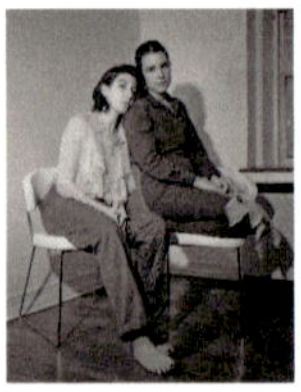

X 40 SOPHIE + ISABEL EARLY (2020?) LATE (2019)

2019.12

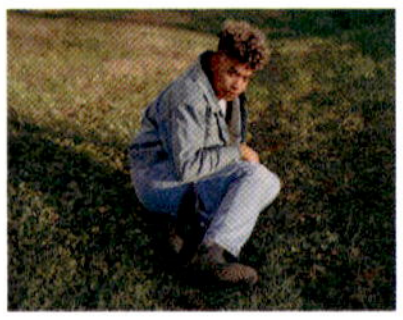

41 EVA (2019)

I THINK WE MET ONLINE FIRST? FIRST IN-PERSON MEET, 3RD ATTEMPT

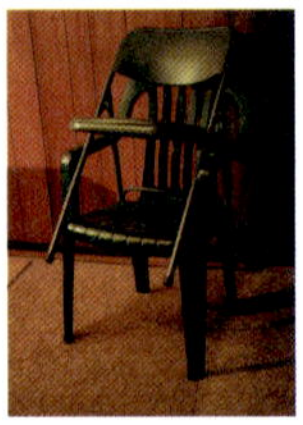

X 42 CAROL'S BASEMENT (2019)
(IF MY PARENTS BELIEVED IN GODPARENTS, SHE WAS THAT)

MICHIGAN SCANS

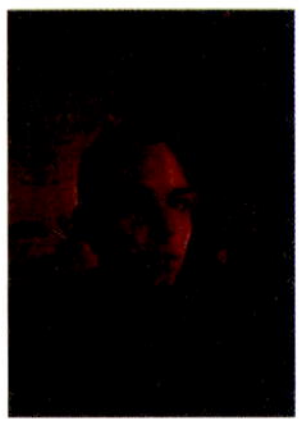

43 SELF PORTRAIT (2017)
(I THINK THIS WAS THAT HOUSE ON WILKENSBURG WHERE I SLEPT WITH ZAY IN A TWIN BED FOR ALMOST A YEAR)

INDEX 06

X 44 JENNA ON FLOOR (2019)

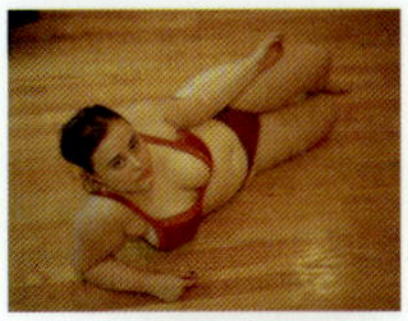

OLD NEEDTFILE

45 SALVADOR AFTER WORK IN THEIR LIVING ROOM (2020)

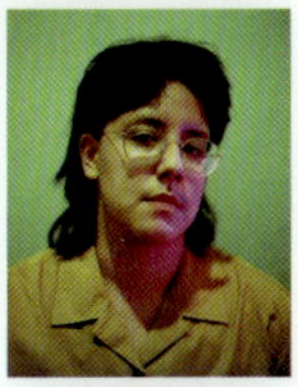

X 46 GEEP BEHIND THEIR HOUSE IN THE COLD ~~(2018)~~ 2019

2019.01

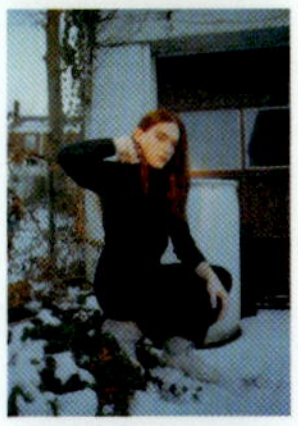

47 SHANNON IN WINTER BEFORE THE SUMMER ~~LATE (2017?) 2016?~~ 2018

2020.05 ~~edit22~~ edit15

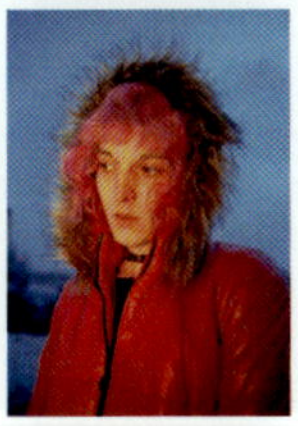

X 48 MOM (2018)

2018.09

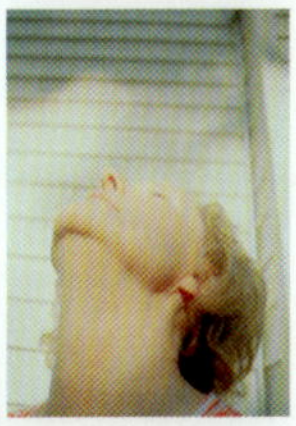

X 49 ARI IN THE WET GRASS (2020)

2020-09

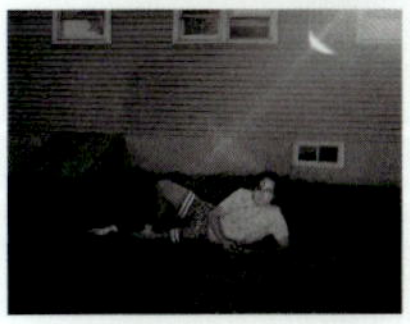

X 50 ELLA IN OUR LAST SUMMER (2018)

2018.10

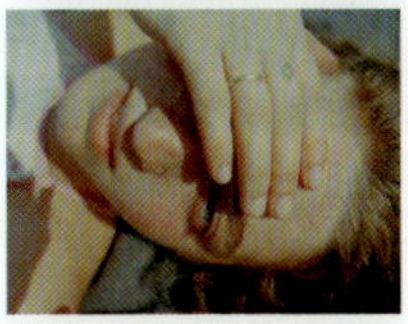

MICHIGAN SCANS

X 51 TRANSTAPE™ (RIPPING THIN SKIN) (ALEEM) (2019)

2019.09

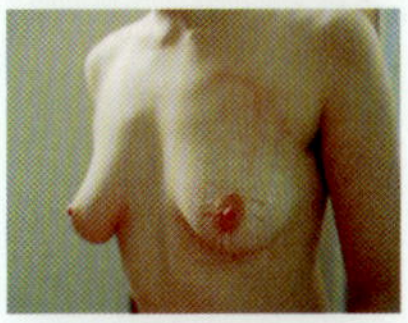

X 52 TAY ON MY WAY HOME (2020)

2020.09

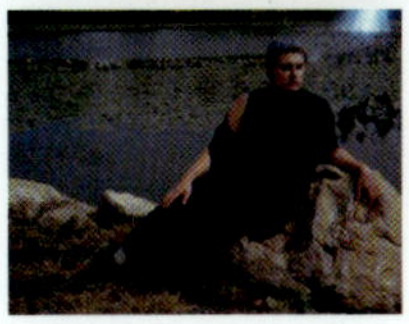

INDEX 07

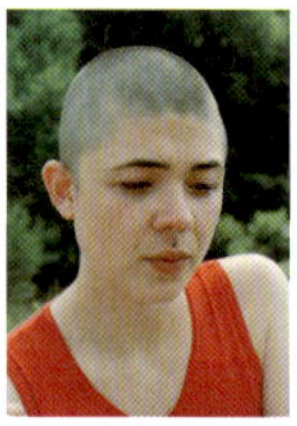

X 53 SOMETHING IN THEIR EYE (2018)
2021.06 (SAME PLACE RACHEL WAS BASKING)
lex28.jpg

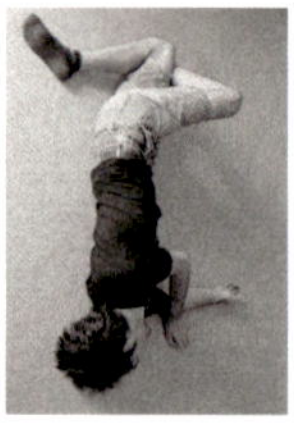

54 ████ BRAN ~~(2020 OR~~ (2021) ~~(2020)~~ (2019)
(IN THE BASEMENT)
2019.09
MICHIGAN SCANS

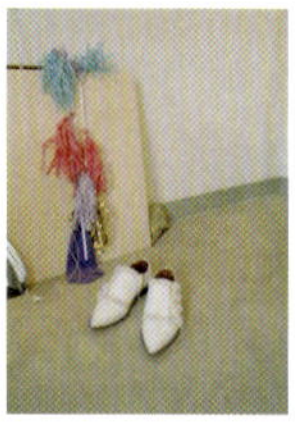

X 55 SUMMER'S ROOM (2018)
(EX-GIRLFRIEND'S SHOES) [WITH written above "EX-"]
OLD PIC NEED

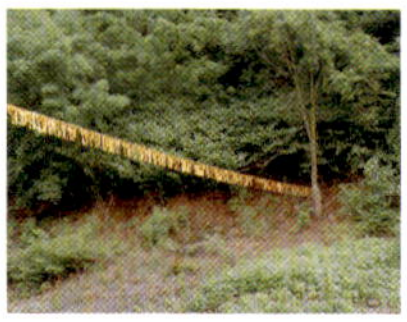

X 56 GRAND OPENING ~~(2017)~~ (2019)
2019.06
landscape01.jpg

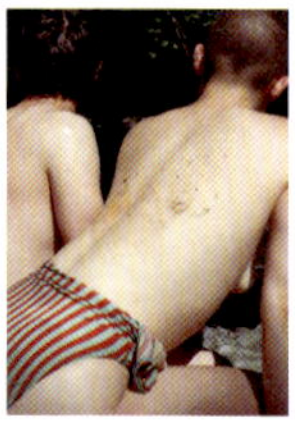

X 57 THE SIDE OF CHRIS AND (2020)
ALEEM'S BACK
BOTH TOPLESS
2020.06

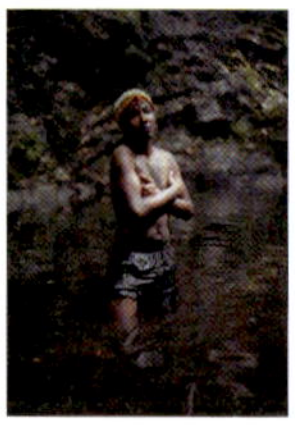

X 58 JUSTICE IN THE HUDSON (2020)
2020.09
justice009

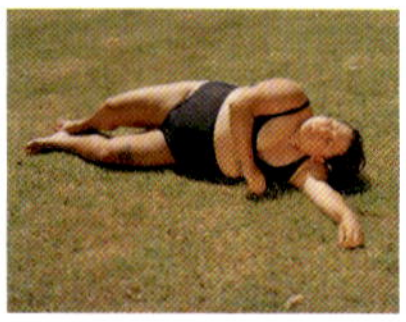

X 59 PROVVIDENZA (IN THE PARK)
(2019)
2019.07

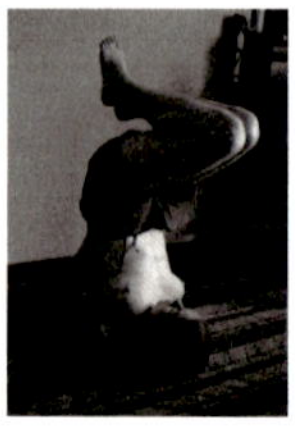

MICHIGAN SCANS
X 60 ALEEM TUCKING + ROLLING (2019)
IN OUR MOTEL ROOM
2019.09

THANK YOU—

ROSS, FOR SHOWING ME EVERYTHING
PHOTOGRAPHY COULD BE, FOR HELPING
ME START THIS WORK 8 YEARS AGO

ALEEM, FOR BEING THERE EVERY DAY,
IMPORTANT OR NOT, FOR LETTING ME
PHOTOGRAPH YOUR BODY AS IF IT WAS MY
OWN, FOR BUILDING A WORLD WITH ME
THAT WE WANT TO EXIST IN, FOR BEING MY
OTHER HALF

SILVER EYE CENTER FOR PHOTO (DAVID, KATE,
SEAN), FOR ALWAYS CHAMPIONING WORK
FROM A REGION OFTEN FORGOTTEN

ELANA, FOR THE COUNTLESS TIMES YOU'VE
LET ME LEAN ON YOU WHEN I WOULDN'T ASK,
FOR YOUR GUIDANCE & FRIENDSHIP

ZAY, FOR ALL THE TIMES YOU PRESSED
THE SHUTTER WHEN I COULDN'T

EDP, FOR CHALLENGING MY ASSUMPTIONS
AND ALWAYS PROVIDING NEW WAYS OF LOOKING
AT THE WORLD, FOR ALL THE WAYS YOU
SUPPORTED ME AS I FOUND A HOME IN NY

ELLA, RACHEL, IAN, TONI, GEEP, NYALLAH,
FOR YOUR CRITIQUE, FRIENDSHIP, FOR EVERY
PORTRAIT YOU SAT THROUGH OR LOOKED AT

STU, FOR SEEING SOMETHING IN THIS
WORK, FOR KEEPING AN OPEN DIALOGUE
OVER THE PAST TWO YEARS THROUGH A
PANDEMIC, TO MAKE THIS BOOK

THE REST OF GOST AND EDS, FOR YOUR
PATIENCE & INTENSE TECHNICAL CAPABILITIES

EACH AND EVERY PERSON, PARTICULARLY
EACH TRANS PERSON, WHO HAS TRUSTED
ME WITH PHOTOGRAPHING YOU, WHO HAS
ALLOWED ME TO USE YOUR IMAGE IN A
NARRATIVE LARGER THAN YOUR OWN.

So what becomes of me,
when I look at an image of myself?

It is

And this is me;
an overbrim of myself

Can it slip out of me
and fall on silver sensitive to light?

Can it spill
to inhabit bodies?
    living or is it quiet?
    Is it tired?

Does it rest
when I rest;
    in an image
    outside my body,

    in a document
that becomes evidence.

My I
    when I confront
an image of myself.

/

Tsohil Bhatia is a transdisciplinary artist currently based in Lenapehoking.
They received an MFA from Carnegie Mellon University School of Art in 2020.

Tuck and Roll
First published in 2023
by GOST Books, London

info@gostbooks.com
gostbooks.com

Edited and designed by GOST:
Rossella Castello, Katie Clifford,
Gemma Gerhard, Justine Hucker,
Allon Kaye, Eleanor Macnair,
Claudia Paladini, Ana Rocha

Printed in Italy by EBS

British Library cataloguing-in-publication data. A catalogue record of this book is available from the British Library.

Isbn 978-1-910401-97-2